CULTURE SMART!
RUSSIA

Mary Habibis

First published in Great Britain 2003
by Kuperard, an imprint of Bravo Ltd
59 Hutton Grove, London N12 8DS
Tel: +44 (0) 20 8446 2440   Fax: +44 (0) 20 8446 2441
www.culturesmartguides.com
Inquiries: sales@kuperard.co.uk

Culture Smart! is a registered trademark of Bravo Ltd

Distributed in the United States and Canada
by Random House Distribution Services
1745 Broadway, New York, NY 10019
Tel: +1 (212) 572-2844   Fax: +1 (212) 572-4961
Inquiries: csorders@randomhouse.com

Copyright © 2003 Kuperard

Fifth printing (revised) 2006

Series Editor Geoffrey Chesler

ISBN-13: 978 1 85733 313 8
ISBN-10: 1 85733 313 6

British Library Cataloguing in Publication Data
A CIP catalogue entry for this book is available from the
British Library

Printed in Malaysia

This book is available for special discounts for bulk purchases for
sales promotions or premiums. Special editions, including
personalized covers, excerpts of existing books, and corporate
imprints, can be created in large quantities for special needs.

For more information in the U.S.A. write to Special
Markets/Premium Sales, 1745 Broadway, MD 6–2, New York,
NY 10019 or e-mail specialmarkets@randomhouse.com.

In the United Kingdom contact Kuperard publishers at the
above address.

Cover image: St. Basil's Cathedral, Red Square, Moscow.
Travel Ink/Dave Saunders

CultureSmart!Consulting and **Culture Smart!** guides have both
contributed to and featured regularly in the weekly travel program
"Fast Track" on BBC World TV.

About the Author

MARY HABIBIS is a writer and trainer specializing in language and culture who has worked extensively with Russian students and teachers. After graduating in psychology and literature at Oxford Brookes University, she worked in language schools internationally for many years before devoting herself full-time to writing. She is the author of a number of textbooks on the teaching of language and cross-cultural communication.

Other Books in the Series

- Culture Smart! Argentina
- Culture Smart! Australia
- Culture Smart! Belgium
- Culture Smart! Brazil
- Culture Smart! Britain
- Culture Smart! China
- Culture Smart! Costa Rica
- Culture Smart! Cuba
- Culture Smart! Czech Republic
- Culture Smart! Denmark
- Culture Smart! Finland
- Culture Smart! France
- Culture Smart! Germany
- Culture Smart! Greece
- Culture Smart! Hong Kong
- Culture Smart! Hungary
- Culture Smart! India
- Culture Smart! Ireland
- Culture Smart! Italy
- Culture Smart! Japan
- Culture Smart! Korea
- Culture Smart! Mexico
- Culture Smart! Morocco
- Culture Smart! Netherlands
- Culture Smart! New Zealand
- Culture Smart! Norway
- Culture Smart! Panama
- Culture Smart! Peru
- Culture Smart! Philippines
- Culture Smart! Poland
- Culture Smart! Portugal
- Culture Smart! Singapore
- Culture Smart! Spain
- Culture Smart! Sweden
- Culture Smart! Switzerland
- Culture Smart! Thailand
- Culture Smart! Turkey
- Culture Smart! Ukraine
- Culture Smart! USA
- Culture Smart! Vietnam

Other titles are in preparation. For more information, contact: info@kuperard.co.uk

The publishers would like to thank **CultureSmart!**Consulting for its help in researching and developing the concept for this series.

CultureSmart!Consulting creates tailor-made seminars and consultancy programs to meet a wide range of corporate, public-sector, and individual needs. Whether delivering courses on multicultural team building in the U.S.A., preparing Chinese engineers for a posting in Europe, training call-center staff in India, or raising the awareness of police forces to the needs of diverse ethnic communities, we provide essential, practical, and powerful skills worldwide to an increasingly international workforce.

For details, visit www.culturesmartconsulting.com

contents

Map of Russia	7
Introduction	8
Key Facts	10

Chapter 1: LAND AND PEOPLE 12
- Geographical Snapshot 13
- The Russian Federation 15
- Russia: A Brief History 18
- Government and Politics 37

Chapter 2: VALUES AND ATTITUDES 40
- Ivan the Fool 40
- Communal Spirit 42
- Patriotism (*Rodina*) 44
- A Pragmatic Attitude to Rules 45
- Openness; Suspicion and Secrecy 45
- Wealth and Money 47
- Hierarchy 49
- Personal Relationships 49
- Attitudes to Women 50
- Smiling 53
- The Good Old Days 54
- Attitudes to Foreigners 54
- Big is Beautiful 56
- *Dusha*—The Russian Soul 56

Chapter 3: FESTIVALS AND CUSTOMS 58
- Holidays and Festivals 58
- The Russian Year 60
- Religion 62

Chapter 4: MAKING FRIENDS 68
- Conversation and Culture 68
- Hospitality and Entertaining 69
- Alcohol 73
- Informality and Openness 75

•	Gifts	77
•	Invitations Home	78
•	Reciprocation	80

Chapter 5: AT HOME   **82**
•	The Russian Family	82
•	The Residence Permit	82
•	*Dachas*	83
•	Cars	84
•	Work	84
•	Everyday Shopping	84
•	Economic Life	86
•	Education	89
•	Military Service	91

Chapter 6: TIME OUT   **92**
•	The *Banya*	93
•	Museums	94
•	Theater and Concerts; Cinema	95
•	Markets; Shopping	96
•	The Kremlin and Lenin's Tomb	98
•	Open Spaces; The Countryside	100
•	The Moscow Metro	101
•	Cultural Programs	102
•	Fun	102
•	Sport	103
•	Eating and Drinking	104

Chapter 7: GETTING AROUND   **106**
•	Hotels	108
•	Apartments	113
•	Taxis	113
•	Car Rental	114
•	Subways; Buses; Trains	116
•	Walking	119
•	Finding Your Way	120

contents

- Clothes   121
- Health   121
- Security   122

Chapter 8: BUSINESS BRIEFING   **124**
- The Russian Economy   124
- The Business Culture   126
- Business Etiquette   130
- Preparing for a Visit   131
- When to Go   133
- Business Meetings and Negotiations   135
- Timing and Punctuality   135
- Seniority in Russian Business   137
- Observing the Hierarchy   138
- Meeting and Greeting   141
- Business Gifts   141
- The Negotiation   143
- How Meetings Proceed   144
- The Importance of Personal Relationships   146
- Managing Disagreement   148
- Interpreting   149
- Contract Finalization   150

Chapter 9: COMMUNICATING   **152**
- Mail; Telephone; The Internet   152
- Finding Out What Is Going On   156
- Greetings   158
- Body Language   158
- Styles of Communication   160
- *Normalno!*   160
- Pride   161
- Swearing   161
- Opening Up   162

Appendix: The Cyrillic Alphabet   **164**
Further Reading   **165**
Index   **166**

Map of Russia

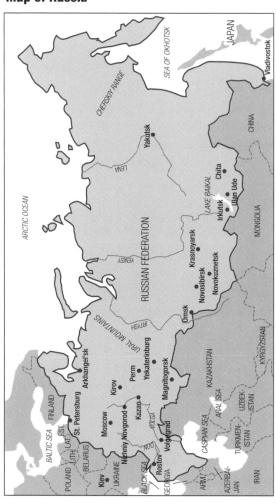

introduction

The Culture Smart! guides set out to equip travelers with human intelligence—vital information about the values and attitudes of the people they will meet, and practical advice on how to behave in unfamiliar situations. If you are visiting Russia, an informed and sympathetic approach is all-important, because for the Russians relationships are everything. Yet the course of its turbulent history has made Russia one of the most enigmatic, complex, and difficult countries for outsiders to decode, despite its power and influence on the world stage and the rich contribution of its art and culture.

The Russian Federation is the successor to the mighty Union of Soviet Socialist Republics that dominated Eastern Europe from the Bolshevik Revolution of 1917 until its demise in 1991. The new order is now over ten years old and it is a good time to ask how Russia has fared.

First of all Russia has lost a lot of territory, as many of the former Soviet republics split off and became independent. These include the Ukraine, the heartland and foundation of Kievan Rus and the breadbasket of the old Soviet Union. They also include Belarus, Moldova, the Baltic states of Estonia, Latvia, and Lithuania, as well as the state of Azerbaijan with its oil capital, Baku. Despite this reduction in size, Russia remains the largest country in the world, and retains its links with much of its former empire as a member of the Commonwealth of Independent States.

Russia today is in a state of flux. The loss of superpower status, the changeover from a highly centralized socialist to a capitalist economy, and the development of new governmental structures have put huge strains on Russian society. They have also reinforced many of its traditional strengths, chief among which is resilience. *Culture Smart! Russia* aims to reintroduce the Russian people to you, their generous qualities of character, what they believe, aspire to, and feel, how they live, how they entertain, and how they conduct business. It offers practical advice, case studies, and illustrative anecdotes to help you forge lasting relationships with this endlessly fascinating country and people.

A Russian visitor to England said, at the beginning of Russia's reopening to the West, "I wonder how long it will be before Russian visitors are two-a-penny and you start to ignore us." The answer, with a people as warm, responsive, different, and important as this, is "Never."

Key Facts

Official Name	The Russian Federation (*Rossiskaya Federatsiya*)	The Russian Federation is a member of the World Trade Organization.
Capital City	Moscow	Population 9–10 million
Major Cities	St. Petersburg (second city); population 5 million	Nizhny Novgorod, Samara, Kazan, Perm, Ufa, Rostov–on-Don, Volgograd, and Novosibirsk.
Area	6,592,800 sq. miles (17,075,400 sq. km)	The biggest country in the world; about one-ninth of the world's total area.
Borders	Norway, Finland, Estonia, Latvia, Belarus, Ukraine, Georgia, Azerbaijan, Kazakhstan, Mongolia, China, and North Korea.	Several former member states of the USSR are no longer contiguous.
Climate	Varies enormously across the huge land area, from the Arctic north to the southerly latitudes of the Black Sea and the moderating maritime influences in the west.	Broadly speaking there is a long cold winter with snow and ice from November to April, a spring thaw from April and May, and a hot summer from June till September.
Time Zones	Russia covers 11 time zones.	Moscow and St. Petersburg are 3 hours ahead of GMT and 8 hours ahead of New York.
Currency	Ruble	

Population	Russia has a population of 147 million, 75% of whom live in cities.	112 million live in European Russia, 35 million live in Siberia and the Russian Far East.
Ethnic Makeup	81% of the population is Slav, but there are significant minorities.	Minorities incl. Tatars, Ukrainians, Chuvash, Belarussians, Bashkirs, Chechens.
Language	Russian	Other languages are also spoken in the autonomous republics.
Religion	Russian Orthodox Christianity	Other religions: Islam, Buddhism, Judaism, and non-Orthodox Christianity.
Government	Multiparty democracy with an elected executive president and a bicameral legislature.	There are 89 administrative areas, with varying degrees of local autonomy.
Media	The main newspapers are *Pravda, Izvestia,* and *Kommercant.* The Russian news agency is TASS.	
Media: English Language	*Moscow Times* and *St. Petersburg Times.* Many hotels have international satellite services.	
Electricity	220v and a standard two-pin plug	Adaptors needed for US appliances
Video/TV	PAL/SECAM system	NTSC TV does not work in Russia.
Telephone	The code for Russia is 007. Moscow's code is 095; St. Petersburg's is 812.	To dial out of Russia, dial 8 (for outside the city), then 10, followed by the country code.

chapter one

LAND & PEOPLE

Welcome to Russia, the largest country in the world. With a landmass greater than the whole of North America and most of Western Europe combined, it has a population of 147 million people, 81 percent of whom are Russian speaking. It is also home to some two hundred sublanguages and a variety of ethnic minorities.

Russia has always proved a difficult country to write about, because of its vastness, its variety, and its unpredictability. Winston Churchill described it as "a riddle, wrapped in a mystery, surrounded by an enigma." The Russians today describe their country as being "in transition." The changes they see taking place are as interesting to them as they are to us, and a lot more personally threatening. Many people long for the certainties of the past—a job, healthcare, a minimum wage, a pension—but few would wish to go back to the stifling political climate of the Communist era. Only the youngest Russians, those in their early twenties, will not have been affected at least in some way by the previous political regime, and even their attitudes will have been indirectly shaped by it.

GEOGRAPHICAL SNAPSHOT

Russia is noted for its harsh climate: bitterly cold winters and short, extremely hot summers. The Russians themselves embrace the winter—its crispness, its beauty, the opportunities for new activity—and prepare for the cold with warm clothes, central heating, and winter tires on cars. The climate has partly given rise to the idea of the stoic, long-suffering Russian, but as a friend once said, "Your image of the downtrodden Russian trudging through the snow looking down is actually the intelligent Russian, checking the sidewalk in front of her, making sure she doesn't slip on the ice."

While there are mountains in the far east and southeast, the main physical feature is a vast, continuous plain stretching from west to east, intersected by the Ural Mountains. The northern countryside is treeless tundra and marshland, where winter dominates for all but five months of the year, with short days, frigid temperatures, and biting winds. For three weeks during June in the north it is light all day and all night—what the St. Petersburgers call the "White Nights." South of this area is a great belt of coniferous forest, and further south are the steppes—rolling grasslands that extend across the continent to Manchuria.

Broadly speaking, Russia west of the Urals is the part best known to the world. It includes the capital, Moscow, and the second city of St. Petersburg. Moscow is on the same latitude as Hudson Bay in Canada. To the south of Moscow is the fertile "Black Earth" country, bordering the Ukraine, with Voronezh as its central city.

The central part of Russia, east of the Urals, is Siberia, a huge area of tundra and steppe with isolated settlements and some major towns, such as Yekaterinburg and Irkutsk. Conditions are harsh almost year-round here, with winter lasting from October to April. Siberia is thought of as always cold, but temperatures rise in the short summer to between 77°F and 95°F (25°C and 35°C).

East of Lake Baikal is Eastern or Pacific Russia, home to many of Russia's Asiatic minorities, living on the steppe and in the semidesert near the Mongolian and Chinese borders. The average winter temperature in Vladivostok, Russia's most easterly city, is 9°F (minus 13°C).

THE RUSSIAN FEDERATION

Present-day Russia is the successor state to the Soviet Union, which collapsed in December 1991. At the same time a number of the former Soviet republics became independent. The new Russia remains linked with these (excluding the Baltic states of Lithuania, Estonia, and Latvia) in a loose Commonwealth of Independent States (CIS). The eleven member states of the CIS include Russia, the Ukraine, Moldova, Belarus, Armenia, Azerbaijan, Georgia, Kazakhstan, Uzbekistan, Kyrgyzstan, and Tajikistan.

The Russian Federation, as Russia is now called, is potentially one of the richest countries in the world, with huge resources of oil, natural gas, timber, and precious metals. Although oil has been exploited since before the 1917 Revolution, major discoveries in western Siberia in the 1960s have allowed Russia to sustain considerable economic growth and aided the rapid transition from a state-controlled to a market economy. Although a small minority has done very well out of the changes, the majority of Russians have experienced great economic hardship.

In terms of its administration, the Russian Federation divides into two main areas, Western or European Russia, which extends from its borders with Finland to the Ural Mountains, and Eastern or Asiatic Russia, which extends to the

Pacific coast at Vladivostok and incorporates the island of Sakhalin and the Kuril Islands. Moscow and St. Petersburg are in European Russia, and so is 75 percent of its population. Eastern or Asiatic Russia further divides into Siberia, which on its own is bigger than the United States, and Russia's Far East, which incorporates the Pacific rim. In addition there are the predominantly Muslim republics in the south.

Moscow and St. Petersburg have populations of 10 million and 5 million respectively. Several other cities have populations of up to 1.5 million. Many Russian cities were renamed after the Revolution in 1917, in some cases several times, and have now largely reverted to their original pre-Communist names. This may cause confusion to visitors who knew Russia before 1991. Street names have also, in most cases, reverted to pre-Communist times. The central shopping street of Moscow, formerly Gorky Street, is once again Tverskaya Street. Old habits die hard though, and don't be surprised if you ask for a particular street and find Russians using its Communist-era name.

Although Russia's economy is buoyed by oil and gas revenues, the country has experienced a fall in living standards as a result of hyperinflation: prices rose steeply following the move to a market economy between 1991 and 1993, and the collapse of the ruble in 1998. The failure of the harvest in

1997 meant that grain had to be imported. Within the big cities a consumer economy has been established, with all the trappings of international fashion and a credit card revolution to match, but this has not yet been replicated across the country. Russia's east coast, however, has benefited from investment and trade with Korea and Japan.

The 1990s saw the rise of the Oligarchs, a small group of businessmen who took over the newly privatized industries and turned them into personal fiefdoms, becoming multimillionaires in the process. Some of them are now in jail or have fled the country. The other new, related, social phenomenon was the "New Russian," a type of yuppie, described as having "too much money, little taste, and no sense."

One of the new benefits of the Russian Federation is that cities formerly closed to foreigners, and to most Russians, are now open, and you can go almost anywhere you want, although your entry visa should state your destinations. (Some sensitive locations are still closed to visitors.) Tourist facilities are developing slowly, however, and can be expensive. Moscow is rated one of the most expensive cities in the world for foreigners to live in. To live more as a Russian does and to travel around easily you must learn Russian, and there are plenty of facilities to help you do that.

RUSSIA: A BRIEF HISTORY

Images of Russia are imprinted on our psyche. Names and events— Peter the Great, Catherine the Great, Rasputin, Lenin, Trotsky, Stalin, the Bolshevik Revolution, the Battle of Stalingrad, the Cold War, and *perestroika*—are familiar to all of us, even if we don't know much about them.

Russia, as befits its size, has been a crucible of creativity: in music, Tchaikovsky, Rachmaninov, and Stravinsky; in literature, Tolstoy, Dostoyevsky, and Chekhov; in art, Kandinsky and Chagall; in ballet, the director Diaghilev and the dancers Pavlova and Nureyev. These are international household names, as are the Russian heroes of science, medicine, and space travel, such as Pavlov, Mendeleev, and Yuri Gagarin, the first man in space. This brief overview tries to put into context some of the names and events that have helped to shape Russia's cultural identity.

The Slavs

The Russians are a Slavic people, related to the Slavs of Poland, the Czech Republic, Slovakia, Slovenia, and Bulgaria. The ancestors of today's Russians probably originated in the area of the Ukraine and modern Belarus, settling in western and central Russia between 100 and 800 CE.

Kievan Rus

The first cities were founded as trading posts along the Volga and Dnieper Rivers by Viking invaders from the sixth century CE onward. Novgorod, Smolensk, and Kiev were founded in this way. In 862 the founding of Novgorod, in the northwest, by Rurik of Jutland is considered the origin of the Russian state, and the name "Russia" comes from the Rus, the dominant Viking clan in the settlement of Kiev in the Ukraine. This gave Russia its original name of Kievan Rus and its original capital, Kiev. The Vikings soon assimilated into the Slavic population.

In the ninth and tenth centuries the Russians converted to Christianity. In 988 the Patriarch of Constantinople created a branch of the Orthodox Church in Kiev, which marked the birth of the Russian Orthodox Church. Under Grand Prince Yaroslav (1019–54) Kiev became the metropolitan see of Russia, and enjoyed a golden age of Byzantine splendor.

The Russians adopted an alphabet introduced by St. Cyril, a Greek missionary. Based on the Greek alphabet, the Cyrillic alphabet was later simplified by his brother, St. Methodius. This written form of Church Slavonic became the basis of the Russian Orthodox liturgy.

The Tatar Invasion

The emerging cities of Russia were laid waste by the Mongol, or Tatar, invasions of the thirteenth century. Led by the mighty Mongolian chief Genghis Khan ("Great Leader"), from the area south of Lake Baikal in eastern Russia, the Tatars established khanates throughout southern Russia, and for two-and-a-half centuries exacted tribute from each community or vassal principality through local leaders or native princes. The area ruled directly by Genghis Khan and his grandson Batu Khan was called the Golden Horde. Beyond it, Mongol suzerainty allowed the Russian princes much autonomy.

The Rise of Moscow

A number of Russian princes consolidated power in the areas under their control while paying tribute to the Khans. Alexander Nevsky, Prince of Novgorod, the subject of a film by Sergei Eisenstein, famously defeated the Swedes on the River Neva (near present-day St. Petersburg) in 1240, and the German crusading order of Livonian Knights in a battle on the ice of Lake Peipus in 1242. Prince Dimitry of Muscovy (Moscow) led a coalition of princes against the Tatars and defeated them at the Battle of Kulikovo on the River Don in 1380. For this he was known as Dimitry Donskoy (Dimitry of the Don). This victory established the beginnings of Russian independence from the Tatars and also the emergence of Moscow as the leading Russian city-state.

Over the next century Moscow increased its influence over the other principalities to become Russia's principal state. Ivan III (Ivan the Great, 1462–1505), Grand Duke of Muscovy, was the founder of the tradition of tsarist autocracy. He conquered Novgorod, threw off the yoke of the Tatars, and turned the Russian Orthodox Church into an instrument of state. His son Basil III (1505–33) gradually replaced the ancient princely families (called *boyars*) with low-born civil servants who owed their position to him. In this way centralized control was established over the Russian principalities. A pyramid of power was established with the ruler at the top, running the country through his nobles.

By 1505, with a population of 100,000, Moscow was one of the biggest cities in the world.

Cossacks

"Cossack" was a name to be feared in Russia. Fierce fighters and horsemen, the Cossacks were the remains of the Tatar invaders who had formed self-governing communities in the Don Basin, Kazakhstan, and around the Dnieper River.

The Russian princes gave the Cossacks autonomy in return for military service, and

Cossack armies were responsible for opening up and colonizing Siberia in the seventeenth century. They were also leading figures in peasant revolts in the eighteenth and nineteenth centuries. After 1917 the Cossack armies were disbanded, but some units were revived in the Second World War.

The First Tsar—Ivan the Terrible (1547–84)
The first ruler to unify all the lands of Russia was Ivan IV, Grand Duke of Muscovy and "Tsar of all the Russias." He had himself crowned "Tsar" (from the Roman *Caesar*) in 1547 and married Anastasia Romanovna, from a nonroyal *boyar* family. After her death in 1560 (he believed she had been poisoned), Ivan attacked and defeated the surviving Tatar khanates of Kazan and Astrakhan, and also the rebellious city of Novgorod, so earning the title of "Ivan the Terrible." By his policy of calculated terror against the unruly *boyar* class, Ivan imposed on Russia an autocratic rule that lasted until the twentieth century. His deeds are immortalized in Eisenstein's film *Ivan the Terrible.*

After a period of civil war and invasions by Sweden and Poland, stability returned to Russia with the election by the *Zemsky Zobor* (Assembly of the Land) of Mikhail Romanov, son of the

Patriarch of Moscow, as Tsar in 1613. The
Romanov dynasty continued to rule Russia until
the Revolution in 1917.

Russia's Development

From the tenth to the sixteenth centuries, Russia
developed from a group of Slavic principalities
paying tribute to a Tatar ruler to an increasingly
centralized state run by an absolute ruler, the Tsar,
based on a peasant economy of landless serfs and
looking inwardly to its own development, with its
own form of Christianity and its own alphabet,
derived from Byzantium. Russia then consisted of
the western cities and the southern Tatar (Cossack)
states. It remained closed to outside influence for
two centuries, evolving separately from Western
Europe. The fact that Russia
did not experience the
European Renaissance had
a significant effect on its
cultural development.

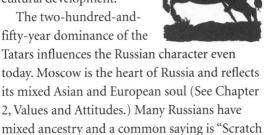

The two-hundred-and-
fifty-year dominance of the
Tatars influences the Russian character even
today. Moscow is the heart of Russia and reflects
its mixed Asian and European soul (See Chapter
2, Values and Attitudes.) Many Russians have
mixed ancestry and a common saying is "Scratch
a Russian and you'll find a Tatar."

Peter the Great (1689–1725)

Six foot seven inches tall (2.2 meters), and with a mercurial character and a ferocious temper, Tsar Peter "the Great" dragged Russia toward the West. After a "fact-finding" tour of Germany, the Netherlands, England, and Austria in 1696–98, he forcibly introduced Western European civilization into Russia, and raised her standing among the European powers. In 1703 he built a new, elegant "European" capital, St. Petersburg, on the marsh at the mouth of the River Neva, newly conquered from Sweden. To pay for its construction he imposed huge taxes, including one on all adult males who refused to shave off their beards!

The founding of St. Petersburg symbolizes a profound contradiction in the Russian psyche. It is a wholly Western city, looking out to the Baltic and beyond. Moscow, to the south and inland, seems closer to Russia's Asian heart (although undeniably European in its location, appearance, and operation). Russians have referred to St. Petersburg as Russia's head, Moscow as its heart.

Catherine the Great (1762–96)

The Empress Catherine was the German wife of the weakling Romanov Peter III, whose throne she usurped. Famous for her lovers, her love of art, architecture, and literature (the Hermitage art collection in St. Petersburg dates mainly from her time), she sought the company of writers of the Enlightenment such as the Frenchman Voltaire, who spent time at her court. While serfdom and misery increased for the peasants, she turned St. Petersburg into one of the most sophisticated capitals in Europe, encouraging the education of a Westernized intellectual elite, alienated from most Russians but also critical of central authority. It was this *intelligentsia* that would in time come to demand social reform and civil liberties. With her chief minister and lover, Count Grigori Potemkin, Catherine extended Russia's territories to the west and the south, taking control of the Crimea and also Lithuania, Belarus, and western Ukraine.

Napoleon (1812)
The Emperor Napoleon of France invaded Russia in 1812 with a Grand Army of 600,000. He defeated the Russians at the Battle of Borodino and entered Moscow unopposed, but was ultimately defeated by the rearguard actions of the Russian army, Cossack guerrilla attacks, and, above all, by the terrible Russian winter. Retreat

turned into rout, and Napoleon left behind 400,000 dead and 100,000 prisoners. This disastrous campaign destroyed his reputation for invincibility and cost Napoleon his mastery of Europe, contributing to his defeat at Waterloo in 1815. His retreat is commemorated in the *1812 Overture*, composed by Tchaikovsky in 1880.

The Decembrists (1825)

In December 1825 a group of disaffected Russian officers in St. Petersburg attempted to overthrow Tsar Nicholas I and replace him with his brother Constantine. They were defeated by loyal troops and many were executed or exiled to Siberia.

This uprising is important because it was the first cry for change from within the ruling classes (there had been peasant uprisings in the past) and marked a division between "Westerners," echoing ideas from the French and American revolutions, who wanted Russia to develop as a Western European state, and "Slavophiles," who placed their faith in Tsarist autocracy.

The Abolition of Serfdom (1861)

In response to the growing demand for reform by the Russian intelligentsia, serfdom was abolished under Alexanders II and III, and with peasants leaving the land to work in the cities, factories, and railways, industrial life developed.

Agriculture, however, remained backward. The abolition of serfdom encouraged liberal reformers and socialist revolutionaries alike. During this period Central Asia and the Far Eastern port of Vladivostok came under Russian control, and Russia sold Alaska (settled as a trading post in 1784) to the United States for 7.2 million dollars.

The 1905 Revolution

At first the government's policies to develop industry were successful. Then a series of poor harvests, an industrial slump, and hardship in the cities caused by a disastrous war with Japan brought social tensions to the boiling point. On January 22, 1905, a peaceful crowd of 200,000 people marched to the Winter Palace in St. Petersburg to deliver a petition to Tsar Nicholas II demanding better working conditions. They were cut down by his Cossack troops. This massacre, known as "Bloody Sunday," was the last straw. Within a week there were outbreaks of strikes all over the country, including mutinies in the navy.

Eisenstein's film *Battleship Potemkin* celebrates this event. It includes the famous Odessa Steps sequence, showing Tsarist troops advancing on demonstrators in the Ukraine. Activists in Moscow and St. Petersburg set up worker's councils, called Soviets, with representatives chosen by popular acclaim. These became the foundation of the new revolutionary system of government after 1917.

In 1906 the Tsar gave way to popular demand for representation by permitting an elected parliament, or *Duma*. Prime Minister Pyotr Stolypin introduced reforms that allowed peasants to buy large parcels of land. This led to the creation of a class of prosperous peasant farmers, the *Kulaks*.

The 1917 Revolution

When the First World War broke out in 1914, Russia was allied with Britain and France against Germany and the Austro-Hungarian Empire. A series of defeats with huge casualties exposed the ineffectiveness of the Russian government. The war caused intense poverty and hunger, and support for the Tsar drained away. Two alternative power groups developed: the *Duma*, periodically disbanded by the Tsar, which attracted the educated and commercial classes, and which formed a Provisional Government; and the Soviets, which attracted soldiers and factory workers, that now sprang up all over the country. At first these two groups cooperated, demanding the abdication of the Tsar. Nicholas abdicated on March 15, 1917, in the face of the German threat of invasion and a revolt by his own troops.

The Provisional Government, led by Alexander Kerensky, decided to continue the war, which was a huge mistake. This unpopular policy was opposed by Lenin (Vladimir Ilyich Ulyanov), leader of the Bolshevik wing of the Marxist Social Democratic Party, under the slogan "Bread, Peace, Land." On November 6 and 7, 1917, the Bolsheviks seized power in Petrograd (as St. Petersburg had been renamed in 1914), and arrested the entire government. Kerensky escaped to exile, and Lenin became head of government.

In December 1917 the new Bolshevik government signed an armistice with Germany, set up a secret police force (the CheKa, forerunner of the NKVD and the KGB), and founded the Red Army. At the same time the Bolshevik Party renamed itself the Communist Party and moved the capital from St. Petersburg to Moscow.

The Communists, called the Reds after their flag, controlled only a small part of Russia, and by the summer of 1918 soon found themselves under attack. Their opponents, the Whites, were an alliance of disparate anti-Bolshevik groups, supported by Britain, France, Japan, and the U.S.A. Under Leon Trotsky (Lev Bronstein), the Red Army was turned into an efficient and motivated fighting machine. Fearing the former Tsar might become a rallying point for the Whites, the Bolsheviks murdered the royal family at Yekaterinburg in the Urals in July 1918. Controversy has raged ever since about whether they all died or whether one or two escaped. The bitter civil war finally ended in 1921 with victory for the Communists. In 1922 the Union of Soviet Socialist Republics was formed, with Lenin as its head—a multinational, socialist empire based on the borders of Imperial Russia.

Joseph Stalin (1879–1953)

Joseph Stalin was a Georgian (real name, Joseph Dzhugashvili) and Commissar for Nationalities in the first Bolshevik government. On Lenin's death in 1924, he outmaneuvered his charismatic rival Trotsky and became General Secretary of the Communist Party, a position of power and patronage. Stalin set out to transform Russia into a modern, powerful industrial nation through centralized state planning. To feed the growing numbers of workers, he forced the peasants into collective farms *(kolkhoz),* and instituted three Five Year Plans, with the result that by 1939 the U.S.S.R. led the world in industrial output (apart from Germany and the U.S.A.). To enforce his goals, Stalin created a totalitarian state, purging the Party and the country of all who might oppose him. He used the NKVD to keep the population terrorized and extended the practice of exiling dissidents to labor camps by setting up the *gulags,* an acronym of *Glavnoe Upravlenie Lagerey (*Main Administration for Camps). By 1939 over twenty million Russians had been transported to labor camps, of whom about twelve million died. The last camp inmates were released only in 1992, by Boris Yeltsin.

The Great Patriotic War

Stalin signed a nonaggression pact with Hitler in 1939 that secretly ceded eastern Poland to Russia and gave it a free hand in the Baltic. Despite this, in June 1941 Hitler's armies invaded Russia, grinding to a halt only at Stalingrad on the River Volga in 1942, in one of the most savagely fought battles of the war. Like the French in 1812, the Germans were forced to retreat during the freezing Russian winter, the Red Army following them all the way and finally entering Berlin in 1945. Enormous sacrifices were made by Russia during the Second World War—at least twenty-six million died, including a million at Stalingrad.

The Cold War

Following the Second World War, the Soviet Union controlled most of Eastern and Central

Europe through puppet Communist regimes answerable to Moscow. To rival NATO, in 1955 the satellite Communist states were locked into a military alliance with the Soviet Union called the Warsaw Pact. Winston Churchill described the border separating Soviet-dominated Europe from the parliamentary democracies as an "iron curtain." The state of tension between the Soviet Union and the Western powers led by the U.S.A. became known as the Cold War—an ideological and military war with limited armed conflict, but overshadowed by the threat of nuclear weapons.

Glasnost and *Perestroika*

Following Stalin's death in 1953 a collective leadership assumed power in Russia. Nikita Khrushchev introduced a policy of liberalization and denounced the errors and crimes of the Stalin era at the 1956 Party Congress. Despite a conservative backlash in the Party, resulting in a renewal of the Cold War, ordinary people became increasingly aware of the scale of the failures and anomalies of the Communist system—industrial inefficiency, overdependence on the military, lack of personal freedom—and in 1986 the relatively young General Secretary, Mikhail Gorbachev, introduced a number of reforms, promoting *glasnost* (openness) and *perestroika* (domestic, economic, and political restructuring). He also moved to reduce the huge stockpile of nuclear weapons held by the U.S.A. and the Soviet Union, and to withdraw Soviet troops from abroad.

Gorbachev's policy of *glasnost* helped to fan nationalist demands for greater independence among the Soviet republics of the Baltic and Transcaucasia. He responded to these by declaring (through a spokesperson) "the Sinatra doctrine"—letting them do it their way, after the Frank Sinatra song "My Way."

In foreign policy, the Cold War was formally ended at the summit meeting between Gorbachev and President Bush in Malta in 1989, opening up the possibility of GATT membership and Western investment. This move was rapidly followed by the reunification of East and West Germany in 1990. Meanwhile the republics of the U.S.S.R. were beginning to seize on changes being made in the constitution to flex their muscles.

In the largest of the republics, the "reform-communist" Boris Yeltsin took power as President of the Russian Federation, while many of the conquered states began to push for unilateral independence. The first was Lithuania in 1990, and the other Baltic republics of Estonia and Latvia soon followed suit. In 1991 five republics—the Russian Federation, Kazakhstan, Belorussia, Tajikistan, and Uzbekistan—signed a new, more truly federal Union Treaty, replacing the 1922

U.S.S.R. treaty, according to which tax revenues would largely remain in the individual republics, with only a proportion going to Moscow. It was accepted that Estonia, Latvia, Lithuania, Georgia, Armenia, and Moldova would not sign.

The Abortive Anti-Gorbachev Coup

In 1991 an attempted *coup d'état* by the Communist Party old guard, the KGB, and the military was faced down in Moscow by Boris Yeltsin. The hardliners made their move in August, when most Russian politicians are at their *dachas* (country houses), imprisoning Gorbachev in his *dacha* on the Black Sea.

But the plotters failed to arrest Yeltsin, who resisted them as head of a democratic "opposition state" based at the *Duma*, the Russian parliament. The elite Tamanskaya guards remained loyal and formed a defensive ring around the *Duma* building, known as "the White House," just over a mile from the Kremlin. The Ryazan paratroop regiment under General Grachev also supported Yeltsin, who called for a general strike and Gorbachev's reinstatement.

Unable to capture the White House, or win public approval or international recognition, the coup collapsed. Over the next six months Yeltsin, not Gorbachev, became the engine of radical democratic change in Russia. The old Communist structures began to crumble and a new dawn of grassroots capitalism emerged, from trading in Ismailovsky Park to setting up restaurants and canteens in student basements.

The failed coup hastened the disintegration of the U.S.S.R., with some of its constituent republics becoming independent states (Estonia, Lithuania, Latvia, Ukraine, Moldova, Georgia, and Kazakhstan). The Soviet Union was formally dissolved on December 25,1991, when Gorbachev resigned as president, and eleven of the former Soviet republics came together in the Confederation of Independent States (CIS), with Boris Yeltsin as president and prime minister.

In Russia the Communist red flag with its hammer and sickle was replaced by the traditional Russian red, white, and blue tricolor. Russia was now a Federation, and a member of a loose confederation of some of the former republics of the Soviet Union. The new Russian constitution was formally promulgated in 1993.

Up to Date
In 1992 and 1993 the sudden abolition of price controls led to hyperinflation, wiping out people's savings. This, coupled with the devaluation of the ruble, caused a run on the banks and led to poverty and instability. At the same time the Russian parliament was in dispute with Yeltsin's

government over the shape of the new constitution. In October 1993 the armed guard took over the parliament building and the Ostankino TV station. This time it was Yeltsin who forced parliament into submission.

In 1998, for a second time, family savings were wiped out with the crash of the ruble as the consumer boom in the big cities ended. Between August and December 1998, the average Moscow family's income dropped by 75 percent.

Before the crisis, most families were getting by on the equivalent of $400 a month. After the crisis they were existing on $100. Nevertheless, for a minority, the consumer boom did not stop altogether. Although incomes were falling, much of the economic activity was conducted in dollars, which were not affected by the fall of the ruble. The dollar cash economy grew. Since 1998 the Russian economy has grown at an average of 8 percent a year, largely due to the power of the Russian oil and gas industry.

In 1994 and again in 1998 Russian troops clashed with activists in the republics of Dagestan and Chechnya, which were seeking complete independence, leading to long and difficult war of containment by the central government. Yeltsin resigned as president in 2000, nominating

Vladimir Putin as his successor. Putin went on to win the subsequent presidential election.

At present, power and money is concentrated in Moscow, but one shouldn't underestimate the power of the regions, especially with the independent attraction of foreign investment. This is particularly the case in the Volga region with the growth of Saratov, Samara, and Voronezh, and the growth of Japanese and Korean investment in Russia's Far East, notably in Vladivostok.

GOVERNMENT AND POLITICS

Russia is still emerging from the seventy-year experiment of Communism. As recently as 1989 it was ruled by the Communist Party of the Soviet Union, under a Politburo and a General Secretary, who was effectively the nonelected president of Russia. Before that, up until 1917, it had been an absolute monarchy ruled by the Tsars.

This is a very short time in which to build functioning democratic institutions, and it is important to understand the huge changes that Russia is coming to terms with in her constitution and system of government. You may hear some people wish for the security and certainty of the old days, but for all Russians a return to the past is not possible. The country as a whole is committed to the new democratic system.

The structure of the government is set out in the constitution of 1993. There is an elected executive President and a bicameral legislature, the *Duma*. The President is head of state and appoints all ministers, including the Prime Minister, who is effectively number two in the government. All ministerial appointments must be approved by the *Duma*. Presidential elections are held every four years.

The upper house of parliament has 178 seats and is called the Federation Council (*Soviet Federatsii*). It is unelected and seats are occupied by two representatives from each of Russia's eighty-nine administrative districts plus Moscow and St. Petersburg. The prime responsibility of the Federation Council is the relationship between the central government and the regions.

The lower house of parliament, the State *Duma* (*Gosudarstvennaya Duma*), has 450 members and is responsible for economic legislation. Half of its members are elected from single-member districts, and half from party lists. Elections are held every four years. A hundred and fifty political parties, blocs, and movements registered to be eligible for the December 1999 elections, of which thirty-six actually qualified to participate. Because of the plethora of political parties, Russian governments have been coalitions. The Communist Party is the largest single party in the country, but it is not part of the ruling coalition. Although it still contains some old elements, it has completely reinvented itself to participate in a democratic system. A special Constitutional Assembly continues to be responsible for the evolution of Russia's 1993 constitution.

Regional Politics

The Russian Federation has eighty-nine administrative areas, broken down into forty-nine *oblasts* (regions), six *krays* (administrative territories), twenty-one independent republics (set up largely to allow ethnic self-determination, although the population in many of them is Russian), two federal cities (Moscow and St. Petersburg), ten autonomous *okrugs* (districts or counties within the regions or territories), and one autonomous *oblast*. The republics have their own constitutions and assemblies, and elect their own presidents. The other administrative areas are run by an elected governor and send representatives to the *Duma* in Moscow.

Broadly speaking, central government deals with defense and long-distance communications, while local government deals with local services and privatization. However, President Putin has appointed seven super-governors, responsible for the smooth running of their regions, which suggests increased control by central government.

chapter two

VALUES & ATTITUDES

History and geography have left their mark on the Russian character. Centuries of permanent military threat have given the Russians a special sense of patriotism—hence the sobriquets of "Holy Russia" and "Mother Russia" you can still hear today. The severe climate has led to the necessity of living and working together, creating a spirit of cooperation, and the vast size of the country is reflected in the Russian preference for doing everything on a large scale.

Although these may sound like generalizations, certain features of the national character are undeniably evident. The Russians, like all of us, are deeply affected by their background.

IVAN THE FOOL

Folktales tell us a lot about a society's view of the world and its moral values. Generally, archetypical folk heroes are strong, handsome supermen who, often aided by supernatural powers, save their people from various forms of evil—dragons, monsters, or hostile armies. Russian folklore has its share of this sort of action hero.

However, the best-loved hero of Russian folklore is Ivan-Durak, or Ivan the Fool. Unlike his clever, ambitious, successful brothers, Ivan is the very opposite of heroic. Small, meek, and shabbily dressed, he is mocked by the worldly people around him. He does not seek fame or fortune and declines all offers of advancement. However, at the end of all such stories it is he who wins the princess and gains the kingdom.

Ivan's power lies in his simple, pragmatic, and generous nature. He gives his last piece of bread to a hungry she-hare and later she, also being the humblest creature in her world, helps him to destroy a monster. The fact that nobody takes Ivan seriously makes him strong. He is naive, compassionate, reticent, and without guile. Dismissed as a fool, to the people he is a hero.

The character of Ivan-Durak gives us the key to understanding the Russian mentality. It suggests that people who may not have an imposing appearance or manner may nevertheless be deserving of respect. Boris Yeltsin shares some similarities with Ivan the Fool, as did Nikita Khrushchev in the 1960s. The contrast with certain Western styles of leadership—appearing confident, outgoing, and permanently in command of any situation—will be obvious.

COMMUNAL SPIRIT

The communal spirit is one of the most typical features of Russian life. For centuries Russia's peasants, until the early twentieth century the majority of the population, lived in village communes called *mir* or *obshchina.* The community united and defended the peasants from the outside world, from foreign invaders, bandits, landlords, and the state bureaucracy.

Community problems were dealt with in a general meeting: how much land should be given to a particular family, who needed communal aid, who must go to war, how to pay taxes, how to punish guilty members. Even family problems, in the case of a serious dispute, might be discussed at a general meeting. This system of cooperation did not let the poor fail, and it did not let the rich rise too much either.

Thus, despite the widespread resentment of Communist rule after the 1917 Revolution, the ethos of collectivism, social equality, and egalitarianism had always been part of Russian social life. It had existed long before Communism was introduced, and even today the *kolkhoz,* or collective farm, is still a common form of organization in many regions of Russia's countryside. Under the circumstances, the principle of mutual assistance is even more vital than the instinct of self-preservation.

United Against Authority

In a characteristic Russian scenario, cars tear along an expressway, breaking all the speed limits. Suddenly cars coming from the opposite direction begin to flash their headlights. A Russian driver reacts at once, slowing down as he understands that traffic police are ahead. He passes them at the proper speed, and then immediately rushes forward at his previous high speed, flashing his headlights to warn other drivers. Law-abiding Westerners may regard this kind of behavior as reckless, bordering on hooliganism, and a potential danger to other people. Russians consider it to be an example of solidarity, friendly relations, and mutual assistance.

Communal Solidarity

Among themselves, the Russians prefer to collaborate rather than compete. This inborn spirit of solidarity may militate against Western ways of doing business. For example, the advertising campaign of a well-known soft drink brand included a competition with prizes for those who collected bottle tops with certain matching designs. Immediately in Moscow, St. Petersburg, and elsewhere spontaneous markets sprang up where collectors came together to pool their bottle tops in order to get the prize.

Communal Responsibility

The downside of this spirit of collectivism is that Russians take the liberty of interfering in the affairs of their acquaintances, neighbors, and even strangers in the street.

Foreigners living in Moscow with their families are invariably surprised by intervention from complete strangers: if you are out with a child in cold weather and the child is hatless or, from the Russian point of view, too lightly dressed, be prepared for a shower of advice or reproach for being too casual, not concerned about your child's health, etc. Giving advice to complete strangers, whether foreign or Russian, is a Russian habit.

PATRIOTISM (*RODINA*)

Another distinctive feature of Russian life is national pride. The Russians are intensely patriotic and view their country almost as a living being. On the other hand, they constantly complain about it. Do not be encouraged to join in if you hear statements like: "It is impossible to live in this country!" The Russians often complain about their own way of life (indeed, there are enough grounds for it), but they don't appreciate the same kind of criticism from strangers.

A PRAGMATIC ATTITUDE TO RULES

Foreigners tend to think of Russia as a society dominated by regulation. In many ways it is, but that doesn't mean you have to obey all of the rules. The attitude of Russians to laws, rules, and instructions is complicated. For instance, walking in a Moscow park in a heavily populated district, you will certainly see signs saying "No dogs! Penalty…" Beneath these signs there will be dozens, even hundreds, of dogs doing what dogs do. Under the circumstances the "Forbidden" signs are absurd and need not be obeyed. Once you are aware of this attitude to rules and regulations, you will not be surprised to see students smoking happily under a "No smoking!" sign, or hear people ask the price of alcohol at a kiosk displaying a "Not licensed" sign. This kind of knowledge can be vital for visitors to Russian cities. For instance, pedestrian crossings are ignored in cities in spite of the rule.

OPENNESS

Although Russian relationships are apparently closed to strangers, with people they know, they are characterized by great openness. Relations among people are informal and friendship is valued very highly. Be prepared for a long and detailed answer to the question "How are you?"

The standard reply of foreigners, "Fine, thanks" may well upset Russians. Westerners will conceal or hint at their real emotions in a social exchange. A Russian will tell you straight out.

Foreigners are invariably astonished or even shocked by their openness. The Russians are not good at formal small talk. Consequently, do not be surprised if during a night's train journey from Moscow to St. Petersburg complete strangers who happen to be in the same compartment with you will tell you intimate details of their private life.

Communication in Russia, even in the course of business, is always very personal. Questions about your private affairs, emotions, and the state of your heart and soul are as customary as life stories. The Western convention of talking about the weather as a way of breaking the ice or measuring someone's mood is not sufficient for most Russians. They may also be offended by the Western custom of sending ready-made cards. A Russian friend once said how, after a long silence, she received a letter from her American acquaintances. She was was deeply hurt when she opened it to discover a "Happy New Year" card with the signature "Anne and John." A printed card is regarded as a sign of neglect. It means that the senders could not find the time to write even a few words about their life, work, and family. That is what a Russian expects from correspondence.

SUSPICION AND SECRECY

Russian openness, however, lives side by side with suspicion and secrecy. Here is a simple but illustrative example. Picking wild mushrooms is a national sport in Russia, where mushrooms are considered to be a delicacy. When returning from the woods, mushroom-pickers usually try to cover their baskets with leaves and twigs. The idea behind this is: "Other people should not know how much we have gathered. If we have many mushrooms they will run to the woods and discover our mushroom places, or they will envy and dislike us. If we have few mushrooms, they will laugh at us because we do not know how to find mushrooms." Being naturally cautious and secretive may lead a Russian to an involuntary deception, or to make simple procedures unnecessarily complicated.

WEALTH AND MONEY

The Russian attitude to wealth and money is also extremely complicated. Russian culture and literature have always taught that wealth does not bring happiness. History gives striking examples of this. By the second half of the nineteenth century, some Russian merchants and industrialists had become very rich, and their entrepreneurial and business talents were widely acknowledged. However, a feeling of guilt about the possession of so much wealth made them spend abundantly on churches, schools, hospitals, or various charities.

Their children and grandchildren spent their wealth on art and culture: they created great collections of works of art, financed folk crafts, opened new theaters, and supported young, talented artists. Merchant dynasties such as the Morozovs and Mamontovs were brought to bankruptcy by their patronage of the arts and charity activities. For these nineteenth-century Russian businessmen, saving money for its own sake was pointless.

Today in Russia wealth may cause envy or breed ill feeling ; it does not bring respect. This upsets the "New Russians" who, despite their millions, have failed to earn respect in Russian society.

Choosing the Right Moment

It is no secret that bribery is a way of solving a number of problems in Russia, but choosing the wrong time, or doing things the wrong way (being too obvious), may offend people. You will find that the popular Russian principle of "poor but proud" is often more important than any money offered.

HIERARCHY

Relations within the social structure are complex. On the one hand, there is a strict hierarchy in Russian society, respect for those who are superior, and deference to their authority. The family is by tradition paternalistic and authoritarian, and this relationship has extended to business and the state. At the same time, the way people speak to each other sounds much more egalitarian and informal. Generally, relationships between bosses and employees come across as being less formal and more humane than in other countries. Part of this is due to the respect for the "little person" described in many works of Russian literature. Even a tiny screw going wrong in a big machine may stop its functioning. Russian people do not forgive and forget disrespect, even if you are a boss or have a lot of money.

PERSONAL RELATIONSHIPS

Russia's is a relationship-oriented society. A polite request instead of an order can perform miracles. Very often attention and respect are more important to people than money and career. No wonder that in Russia a person may describe a boss they like as "respectful," "attentive," or "nice."

Bring little souvenirs from your country to give as tokens of appreciation for a person's work or cooperation. You might give them to the person on duty in the hotel, a secretary at work, a nurse at a hospital, or a neighbor. A Russian proverb goes, "It is not your present but your love that is dear to me." Attention and kindness are appreciated, not the financial value of souvenirs.

ATTITUDES TO WOMEN

The Russian attitude toward women is more traditional and conservative than in most Western countries. On the other hand, the Russian woman was proclaimed "free" immediately after the Revolution of 1917, and the Soviet state enshrined equal rights for all. Even today, however, the following situation is typical. The wife may have a more prestigious and better-paid job, but it is the husband who is the head of the family and who has the last word. There is a contrast between the Russian ideal of family life, in which the man is master of the household, earns the money, and makes the key decisions, and the modern reality of the Russian businesswoman occupying high positions in firms, banks, ministries, and state institutions. The apparent contradiction can be summed up by the motto, "A career is good but family happiness is better." A businesswoman at home wants to feel supported, but also may expect to be the subordinate figure.

The Evidence of Love

There is a well-known saying that represents old-style family relationships in Russia: "He beats me, so he must love me." This expresses the idea that the true feelings necessary to a strong relationship can sometimes find extreme expression. Jealousy, after all, can be a great affirmation. It's also a reflection of the traditionally subservient position of the Russian woman.

This kind of relationship, however, is no longer typical of family life in modern Russia. Like so much else in Russian society, things are changing fast, which may well be a factor in the very high divorce rate in the country today.

Traditional attitudes to the place of women are reflected in the Russian language. The word for a man, *zhenitsya,* means "to take a woman." A woman is *vyhodit zamuzh*, which literally means "to step behind your man."

However, the Russian woman's search for a strong man doesn't make her a stay-at-home wife. "Homemakers" are a rare breed and exist only in certain segments of society, such as the military, as soldiers move frequently and suddenly from place to place, or among "New Russians," for whom a nonworking wife at home is a social trophy. The majority of women work full-time, not just for financial reasons but also because they are eager to use their skills and talents, to do something useful and important.

The Russians love children and family values are still very important. Unmarried men and women often arouse suspicion: something must be wrong with them. Single women sometimes suffer from an inferiority complex. An unmarried career woman, a Russian academic, earning a good salary, refused to go to a meeting of her colleagues because "They will ask questions about my husband and children and I have nothing to say."

The relations between the "strong man" and "weak woman" are something of a game in modern Russian society, but both sides play it assiduously. In the streets and in public places, courtesy to women is seen to be important: men expect to open and hold the door for a woman, give up their seat on public transportation, let a woman pass first, help her on with her coat, and so on, customs that have generally died out in the West.

The game goes on in business relations. Foreign businesswomen often complain that they are not taken seriously because they misinterpret old-style Russian courtesy. Here it is important not to confuse form and content. There are many businesswomen in Russia—in some spheres, such as education and trade, they may predominate. However, certain conventions are still observed. If you are a woman who has come to Russia on business you will receive special consideration from your Russian hosts. They may kiss your hand on introduction or departure. They will let you pass first, often with the words in English: "Ladies first." At a party where a woman is present there will be the inevitable toast "to fair ladies." Attentiveness to women, hints of flirting, are acceptable at business meetings in Russia. This is not condescension but appreciation.

SMILING

The Russians have often been described as a "melancholy, unsmiling people." This is not true. They are not at all gloomy, but traditionally they do not smile at strangers. To do so might be regarded as a sign of stupidity. A Russian proverb says, "Laughter for no reason is a sign of foolishness."

When the first McDonald's was opened in Russia, the staff were specially trained to smile at clients. This caused some difficulties because, as a young Russian man put it, "Customers will think that we are utter fools."

The Russians reserve their smiles for people for whom they have good feelings.

THE GOOD OLD DAYS

The Russians do not like talking about politics to strangers. Concepts such as democracy, capitalism, and freedom may have different connotations for them, and give rise to misunderstanding. For example, a political label stigmatized in the West may actually describe an excellent businessman, a reliable partner, and an intelligent and sympathetic person. In the same way, someone who feels nostalgic for the good old days of Communism may simply be looking back to the lost security of a guaranteed job, cheap food, and free medical care. Russian politics is very complicated; it is not just black-and-white as it is presented in the West. Therefore during your talks leave your preconceptions behind.

ATTITUDES TO FOREIGNERS

The attitude of Russians to foreigners varies greatly, too. The gap between the generations is more obvious in this respect. Older people who grew up during the years of isolation often regard foreigners with suspicion, sometimes feeling uncertain, embarrassed, and shy. Young people, who are more open-minded and better traveled, show greater interest and curiosity. All age groups share a feeling of pride and independence that can manifest itself as arrogance. Today, as Western influence is becoming more pervasive in everyday life, there is a change of mood in many young people: as well as embracing Western goods and services they are growing more aware of the need to defend their own cultural identity.

On the other hand, the importance of hospitality and the desire to impress foreigners means that Russians will pull out all the stops for foreign visitors. Even in the crisis of the early 1990s, when the country was on the verge of starvation, Russian hosts gave magnificent parties for foreign guests both to show them respect and maintain the traditions of Russian hospitality

Problems can arise, however, from the stereotypical notions that many Russians have about foreigners. One of them is that all visitors from abroad are fabulously rich. In Russia there are usually two prices in hotels, restaurants, and museums: one for Russians and a different one for foreigners. Do not get upset. The dual price system simply takes into account the fact that Russian salaries are very low compared to those of foreigners. It is difficult for people who earn $50 a month to understand the thrift of those who earn ten to a hundred times more. They see it as greed.

A popular phrase from the 1930s goes, "A car is not a luxury but a means of conveyance." In Russia this saying has been adapted to: "An American is not a luxury but a means of conveyance." Indeed, a small number of Russian women look upon foreigners only as a means to emigrate. They are in the minority.

BIG IS BEAUTIFUL

Russia is vast and the Russians like to think big. They like large-scale projects and big numbers. The Moscow McDonald's served 70,000 customers a day when it opened; Aeroflot, the Russian airline, was the largest in the world. The Russian army was the biggest in the world, as was Russia's industrialization program in the 1930s. The Tsar Bell in the Kremlin in Moscow is the heaviest in the world, and the Tsar Cannon has a bore of thirty-six inches and weighs forty-four tons. The bell is too heavy to ring and the cannon is too big to fire. Thinking big is reflected in their radical, sweeping approach to government and to reform.

DUSHA—THE RUSSIAN SOUL

Dusha, the Russian term for "soul," lies at the heart of Russian behavior and is part of everyday life. Ultimately, successful relations with Russian people will be based on mutual liking and emotion. Russians can walk away from a deal if that element isn't present. In the arts, *dusha* manifests itself as emotion, exuberance, flamboyance, sentimentality, energy, and flair. In life, it manifests itself as suffering, even a love of suffering as a purifying process. It is also reflected in the love of nature, the importance of family, and a sense of duty and compassion. An important aspect of *dusha* is *tselnost*—wholeness, or complete commitment.

You can see *dusha* in the Russians' respect for parents, old age, learning, and the primacy of emotions and personal feelings. Their great fear today is that the advent of a more materialistic society will destroy these values. When a Russian invites you to his or her home and you exchange real confidences about yourselves (maybe over vodka) you will have a real relationship, for you will have touched each other's souls.

chapter three

FESTIVALS & CUSTOMS

HOLIDAYS AND FESTIVALS

Russia's official public holidays are still secular rather than religious. There are national holidays and many regional and even city celebrations. On both public holidays and religious festivals shops, places of entertainment, and some public utilities are likely to be closed.

THE MAIN PUBLIC HOLIDAYS	
January 1	New Year's Day
January 7	Orthodox Christmas
March 8	International Women's Day
April/May	Orthodox Easter
May 1–2	May Day, Spring Festival
May 9	Victory Day (World War II)
June 12	Independence Day (from the Soviet System)
November 7	National Accord and Reconciliation Day
December 12	Constitution Day

Holiday Times

August is the traditional summer holiday month in Russia, but the first two weeks in May and the first two weeks in November are also popular.

If a public holiday falls on a Tuesday, then the preceding Monday is also declared a holiday, but the following Saturday is declared a working day.

Weddings

Weddings in Russia can last from two days to a week. The groom collects his bride and they go in a train of cars to the registry office to exchange rings and sign the book (the ring is on the third finger of the *right* hand). The civil wedding may be followed by a church wedding a few days later.

Religious Holidays

Although they are not national holidays, much of the country also celebrates traditional religious holidays such as Good Friday and Easter Monday, All Saints' Day (November 1), and, curiously, the Western Christmas Day (December 25).

Unlike the Western Churches, which follow the Gregorian calendar, the Russian and Greek Orthodox Churches follow the earlier Julian calendar, which generally runs up to thirteen days behind the Gregorian. Thus the Russian Orthodox Christmas falls on January 7 rather than December 25.

THE RUSSIAN YEAR

January 1, New Year's Day
New Year's Day is the major Russian festival now that the old Communist holidays of Revolution Day and International Labor Day have been downgraded. It's quite like Christmas, with carols *(kolyadki)*, gifts, and trees. There's Grandfather Frost with his Snow Maiden, who brings children gifts, and there is traditional food such as *kutya* (berries, poppy seeds, and honey) and *kissel* (a stewed cranberry drink).

January 7, The Orthodox Christmas
Russian Orthodox ceremonies are long and everyone stands throughout. Women are expected to cover their heads and wear skirts of conservative length. You will be struck by the amount of incense burned and the rich vestments of the bearded Orthodox priests, in contrast to their usual black cassocks.

February 23, "Men's Day"
The former Soviet Army Day was always an occasion for families to congratulate their menfolk. It is still very popular today, even though it is not an official holiday any more.

March 8, International Women's Day
This festival celebrates the contribution of women to world culture. However, it does not

reflect the prevailing attitude to women in Russian business culture, which would be described in America and Britain as sexist.

May 1, International Labor Day

In Soviet times this festival used to be celebrated with elaborate parades. Now it is a two-day public holiday.

May 9, Victory Day

This holiday marks the end of World War II and the defeat of Nazi Germany.

June 12, Declaration of Independence

This occasion marks the declaration of Russia as an independent polity within the Soviet Union in August 1991.

November 7, National Accord and Reconciliation Day

Formerly called the Great October Socialist Revolution Anniversary, until recently this holiday marked the coming to power of the Communists in the 1917 Revolution. Once the occasion for huge military parades in Red Square, it has been downgraded.

December 12, Constitution Day

This holiday celebrates the Constitution of 1993 that replaced Russia's Soviet constitution.

RELIGION

In spite of decades of official atheism under the Soviet regime, religion still plays a significant role in Russian life. Broadly speaking there are three kinds of attitude toward religion. There are those people who sincerely believe in God—mostly the elderly, though in recent years young people have joined their ranks. Then there are people who go to church as a fashion statement, or in order to explore the history, roots, and sources of their culture. They are mostly members of the intelligentsia. Finally there are the militant atheists of the older generation, keepers of the flame of the 1930s, when religion was associated with stagnation and backwardness.

Many people who are generally indifferent to religion occasionally go to church, just to be on the safe side, or in times of trouble. (According to a Russian proverb, a Russian peasant will not cross himself until the thunder booms.) Most Russians regard religion as a serious matter and keep their beliefs to themselves. Churchgoing on Sunday for social reasons is not customary. Usually people go to church to pray, sometimes in small groups, more often on their own.

The predominant religion is still Russian Orthodox Christianity. An Orthodox service lasts many hours, and people stand throughout. On entering a church men should take off their hats and women should cover their heads. Light summer clothes, shorts, and sleeveless dresses should not be worn in church; some cathedrals do not admit women in trousers, although the Church has recently become more tolerant of tourists. Naturally, during a service one should not talk loudly, take photographs, film the proceedings, or watch believers too closely.

In recent years the Russians have been carried away by mysticism. Fortune-tellers, healers, and clairvoyants have flooded the country. A hard life encourages all kinds of superstitions. There are even politicians and businessmen who will not embark upon any new venture without consulting their horoscopes first.

The Russian Orthodox Church
The Russian Orthodox Church was founded by St. Vladimir of Kiev, who first introduced Greek missionaries to Russia and then converted to Christianity in 988. It adopted the rituals of Byzantium, but used the Slavic language. In the fourteenth century, when the leadership moved from Kiev to Moscow, the Russian Church established its independence from Greek Orthodoxy. After the fall of Constantinople to the

Turks in 1453, and the defeat of the Tatars in 1480, Russia came to regard itself as the repository of the true faith, the "Third Rome." While the rituals and beliefs of the Russian Orthodox Church have much in common with Roman Catholicism, the Russians do not accept the authority of the Papacy.

The head of the Russian Orthodox Church is the Patriarch, who presides over the churches and congregations of Russia, appoints priests and bishops, and legislates on issues of liturgy and belief. Unlike countries that have established Churches, however, in Russia the Patriarch has no political function. The Orthodox Church is male. There are no women priests or female celebrants, although there are nuns and convents.

After 1917 the status of the Russian Church became very precarious, but the Bolshevik Revolution did not succeed in stamping out belief in Christianity. Officially, the Soviet constitution guaranteed religious freedom, but in reality the Church was controlled by the state. Its priests were persecuted and church treasures and liturgical instruments were destroyed. Religious observance was discouraged, and many churches were turned into barns and pig pens. Churches were forbidden to possess funds, engage in public activity, or teach religion to any person under eighteen. Senior clerical appointments were subject to government approval and supervision, and the Church was used by the state to unify the people at times of crisis.

Since the breakdown of the Soviet system, the Orthodox Church has steadily regained its former position in Russian life. It has come back to fill a void in the lives of its congregations. President Putin is a churchgoer, and former President Yeltsin incorporated the Church into many state functions. The Russian Orthodox Church now runs homeless shelters, provides food, and also organizes orphanages. It is supported by business, and is using its new-found influence to try to ban other religions from Russia.

Other Religious Groups
The Old Believers

Siberia has become a center for numerous dissident Russian Orthodox communities. One group is the Old Believers, who rejected the liturgical reform introduced by Nikon, Patriarch of Moscow, in 1653. They were excommunicated in 1667 and violently persecuted. Many fled to Siberia where their descendants still practice in the area of Ulan Ude.

Western Catholic and Protestant Churches

Non-Orthodox Christian denominations are recognized in Russia, but the opportunities for worship are fairly limited. Western evangelical missionary activity is controversial.

Islam

One of the effects of the breakup of the Soviet Union has been a revival of local Islamic culture, particularly in the traditionally Turkic Russian republics. These are: Adygeya, Bashkortostan, Chechnya, Chuvashiya, Dagestan, Ingushetiya, Kabardino-Balkariya, Karachayevo-Cherkesiya, Khakasiya, Mordoviya, Osetiya-Alaniya (North Ossetia), Tatarstan, and Udmurtiya.

The Traditional Religions of Russia

Shamanism is the ancient religion of Siberia. It was banned in Russia before the 1917 Revolution and was considered to have died out, but is still practiced in Sakha and Buryatia. The Bay of Ayayia and the island of Okhonskh in Lake Baikal are thought to be centers of worhip.

A form of earth worship that dates back to the Stone Age, shaman ceremonies are based on lunar rituals and the worship of ancient sites. All natural objects are believed to have a spirit that can be contacted for guidance, usually through a shaman or medicine man "traveling between the realms." The shaman could also predict the future, determine which days were auspicious for action, and heal disease, using natural remedies.

Buddhism

There are 500,000 Buddhists in the Russian Federation, belonging to the Gelugpa (Yellow Hat) school of Tibetan Buddhism, of which the spiritual leader is the Dalai Lama. Buddhism is mainly practiced by the Buryats and Tuvans and is organized by a Buddhist Religious Board based at Ivolginsk. Lamas are generally trained in Mongolia.

Judaism

Most of Russia's 500,000 Jewish population (there has been a 50 percent decrease since 1989) live in urban western Russia, but a community of 17,000 or so "Mountain" Jews live in the Caucasus.

The Soviets created a Jewish Autonomous Region near the far eastern region of Khabarovsk, centered on the industrial town of Birobidzhan near the Chinese border. This community has been decimated by emigration to Israel, but there is a large Jewish cultural center in Irkutsk.

Grassroots anti-Semitism in Russia has been a strong inducement for Russian Jews to emigrate, especially since *glasnost* and the acceptance of applications for emigration by the government.

chapter four

MAKING FRIENDS

Meeting people and making friends is not difficult in Russia. The Russians value and enjoy being sociable and will chat easily and openly to a sympathetic stranger.

CONVERSATION AND CULTURE

The Russians love books and are better educated in terms of their own culture than many people in the West are in theirs. This includes both literary culture and folklore. Folk stories and songs about the motherland are known to most people, and most children learn the works of the national poet Pushkin at school. It is sufficient for you to show interest in their culture for Russians to share their enthusiasm with you. Conversely, your refusal to take an interest may alienate them.

This may well change as Western pop culture permeates the life of young Russians, and Mexican telenovelas and American soap operas become staples of Russian TV. Nevertheless, the Russians talk about their literary heroes and you should

 know who they are. Russia's period of great literature began in the 1800s, when Pushkin, Tolstoy, and Dostoyevsky were writing. Lermontov's *A Hero of Our Time*, describing his journeys in the Caucasus, is also very popular from this time. In the turbulent twentieth century, Russia produced a number of great poets and documentary novelists. You may find that because of Communist censorship some Russian poets and novelists who are household names in the West, such as Solzhenitsyn, are less well known and less appreciated in Russia.

Patriotism, we have seen, is an important Russian virtue and is quite openly discussed. The city of Moscow has an almost holy significance for many people, especially in the outlying regions of Siberia. The fashionable Western disregard for patriotism may also alienate Russians

HOSPITALITY AND ENTERTAINING

If you go to Russia on business, you will certainly be invited out—whether to lunch in a restaurant or to someone's home. Hospitality is the cornerstone of the Russian way of life. The first and overriding instinct of a Russian housewife is to feed her guests, even if they have dropped in unexpectedly.

For the Russians in general, any informal contact will lead to eating and drinking sitting round the table. However mundane the matter of food may seem, it is socially sensitive and important. For many peoples, the Russians included, a refusal to eat is very offensive.

Stand-up buffets have not caught on in Russia, although major companies and organizations are trying to introduce them into Russian life. The favorite way of establishing contact with people (in business as well as socially) remains sitting around the table, where you can relax, lounge back in your chair, and get down to the serious business of eating and drinking. Even the Russian breakfast tends to be fairly substantial, although business breakfast meetings are unusual. Lunch is the main meal of the day, and less is eaten in the evenings. There is a Russian saying about how to keep healthy: "Eat breakfast alone, share lunch

with a friend, give your supper to your enemy."

The main problem that faces every foreigner visiting Russia is the threat of overeating. The Western term "lunch" corresponds to the Russian *obed* (dinner). However, when guests are to be entertained, supper, which traditionally in Russia is a light meal, becomes a feast. So be prepared for the fact that during the day you may be offered two main meals (lunch and evening) as well as numerous snacks in between.

Snacks, *zakuski,* are basic to Russian entertainment. It is usual to begin with *hors d'oeuvres.* Drinks before a meal are not customary. Foreigners are astonished by the abundance and variety of the *hors d'oeuvres.* These are the Russian housewife's *pièce de résistance.* There are salads, cheeses, cuts of meat, herring, various fish delicacies, caviar, pickles, fresh vegetables and herbs, hot boiled potatoes, pies with savory fillings, and much else. What you may take to be a substantial meal will, as a rule, be only the beginning. It is best to make sure about this right at the start, saying something like, "What a spread! I hope there is not going to be anything else?!" After which, pace yourself.

At lunchtime, the *hors d'oeuvres* are followed by soup. At evening functions soup is often not served, but in the daytime it is a must—most Russians consider that lunch without soup isn't lunch at all! Soup is referred to as the first course.

The second course might include roast meat, chicken (Russians are very fond of chicken, which is not considered an inferior dish), national dishes such as *pelmeni* (meat dumplings), or traditional meat dishes cooked in earthenware pots.

After all this, tea will be served. The Russians are tea drinkers just like the British. Coffee (usually instant coffee) tends to be drunk mainly in the mornings. Desserts— sticky cakes, pies, sweets,

preserves, honey, and so on—are always served together with tea.

Demyan's Fish Soup

There is a popular Russian tale. A man called Demyan invites his neighbor to share his fish soup. The latter declines the offer, explaining that he is stuffed to the gills. Demyan continues to insist, describing the delights of his soup. The story ends on a sad note as the two friends fall out. In Russia, this sort of situation, when you are forced to eat against your will, is known as "Demyan's fish soup." It is a situation you should be prepared for when visiting Russians. Refusal of food for any reason—that you are full, dieting, not used to eating at this time of day—is taken as a slight. The only exception made is for illness. Here you will always be understood. Virtually every Russian considers himself a medical expert, so be ready for a host of questions and advice. There are few things the Russians like better than to discuss medically related topics.

Vegetarians in Russia have a tough time. The Russians like meat and are incapable of imagining a table of festive fare without it. Vegetables are looked on just as trimmings. Spring vegetables and fruit are expensive, and not available in great variety. Because of the severe frosts and economic difficulties, people tend to go for filling foods for energy. Someone who refuses meat is regarded in Russia as a rich eccentric.

ALCOHOL

The Russians are heavy drinkers. Whatever the reason—the cold climate, the wish to create an intimate atmosphere, tradition—this is one stereotype grounded in fact. Despite official crackdowns at various times, drinking is still a way of life in Russia, and a way of making friends. You will be offered vodka and you will be seen as standoffish or "a wimp" if you don't accept. Younger age groups and groups of women may not drink, but for older business colleagues drinking together is seen as a way of cementing relationships or "finding out what you're really made of." Eating is usually accompanied by numerous toasts and refilling of glasses, and it's in the refilling and toasting and emptying that the damage is done. Unlike the West, where people drink a little and often during a meal, in Russia they "down it in one" and drink a lot. Only one excuse seems to be acceptable for declining a drink—a stomach ulcer.

If your constitution allows it, drink with the Russians; if not, pretend to—lift your glass to your lips, and take little sips. If you don't, you may be pestered by demands that you immediately down a glass. Should you decline, even on the grounds of "doctor's orders," your refusal may destroy the atmosphere of trust and goodwill. The traditional question, asked by a drunken Russian demanding that you drink with him, is nothing if not revealing: "Do you respect me?" A refusal in such a situation is tantamount to an insult. Best to pretend you are drinking, or, better still, drink just a little in order to sustain the atmosphere of mutual understanding.

During a meal, particularly on formal occasions when drinking spirits, it is the custom to drink only after a "command" is given in the form of a toast. Without this only fruit juice or mineral water is drunk. In the south, in the Caucasus, they make long, very elaborate toasts, but in Moscow, too, the ritual is strictly adhered to. When proposing a toast you should get to your feet (traditional toasts such as "to peace and friendship" or "thanks to our hosts," or "to your beautiful city" will always win a Russian's heart), clink glasses (this is essential—the only time you don't clink glasses is when you are paying respects to someone who is dead), and drink.

Younger people may be more relaxed, and beer and wine can be drunk at one's own pace.

INFORMALITY AND OPENNESS

What do the Russians talk about socially? They love talking about family and the problems of everyday life; they will be interested to hear about your country, your company, and your impressions of Russia. They appreciate personal candor, about themselves and about you.

Unexpectedly frank conversations about illness, family, and everyday troubles are quite normal. In Russia, to share your woes and your problems means to become friends. There is a limit to your candor, however. If asked for your impressions of Russia, remember not to criticize, even if the Russians themselves make scathing remarks about their country. And, of course, be ready to discuss business in any situation. If your Russian partners are intrigued by a project, they will want to discuss it all the time, everywhere, and whatever their state of sobriety.

The value of this informal approach to business is that it allows you to pick up new information about your partners and to establish the personal contact that is so important for the successful conduct of business in Russia.

The Russians don't go in for polite "social" chat. Be prepared for the possibility that someone who is entirely unknown to you will, during an official function, tell you about his life in intimate detail, and expect the same from you in return. Many Russians find the formality of Western business receptions puzzling: what is the point of it all if one can't relax and have a heart-to-heart? Spontaneity and unpredictability characterize all forms of business in Russia, where a reception is rarely held according to a timetable and will continue until the last guests have left.

Unexpected visits are commonplace. If you've gathered together, are in a good mood, and feel like company—excellent, let's go visiting, even if no one is expecting us. In such a situation, it is best to go with the flow. Rely on your Russian partners and common sense (if your companion is drunk, for instance, it is best to stay at home).

Improvization

A good example of impromptu entertainment took place in St. Petersburg. On the spur of the moment, a university lecturer invited foreign friends home for dinner, but found she had nothing in the apartment apart from bread. No problem! She borrowed some pepper vodka from a neighbor downstairs and some pickled mushrooms and herring from two neighbors upstairs. The meal was homemade and wonderful, and took only a race up and down stairs to prepare!

GIFTS

If you are invited to someone's home, you are expected to bring a gift, or at the very least flowers for your hostess. What is important is not so much the present as the thought. Something small will do: tea (good quality), candy, calendars, tea towels, or a bottle of wine. Be careful when buying drink for there is a lot of fake product around; don't buy from kiosks or small shops.

If your relations with your hosts are informal, a teapot, a mug, or something useful for the home makes a good present. It's the custom to bring small presents for the children of the house. A sweet for a child is more important than a present

for the grown-ups. Finally, if you have nothing else, always bring a bunch of flowers for your hostess. In Russia it is customary to give women flowers, even without a particular reason. It's essential you give an *uneven* number of flowers; even numbers are for funerals only!

A word about superstitions. The Russians are superstitious—the educated, the young, and business people. There are certain practices that everyone tries to follow, just to be on the safe side. Thus, when you visit someone's home, observe the following rules: Don't greet anyone or bid them farewell across a threshold; it means a quarrel. Don't seat thirteen people round a table; it means a death. Don't whistle in the house, or there won't be any money; and if you have spilled the salt, throw a little over your left shoulder and spit three times; otherwise there will be a scandal. There are a great number of such superstitions, so don't be surprised by strange behavior on the part of your Russian friends.

INVITATIONS HOME

Although the temperature outside may be very cold, inside Russian houses and apartments it is almost always warm to the point of overheating.

Expect to remove your outer garments in the hallway, as well as outdoor shoes such as galoshes or waterproof boots. Usually you will be given slippers. Otherwise it is quite acceptable to walk around the house in bare feet, socks, or tights.

It's important not to arrive empty-handed—remember to bring a gift. Casual dress is normal although, depending on the age group, jeans and T-shirts might be considered too casual. On the whole, the Russians are not very etiquette minded, but pointing with your knife or fork while talking is considered very rude.

As we have seen, Russian hospitality dictates that nothing is too good for the guest, even if it breaks the bank, so it is important to try everything and to accept second helpings when offered. To refuse would be an insult.

Vodka, literally, "little water," flows freely at Russian tables, although in an all-women group it may not. Once again, you shouldn't refuse when someone refills your glass. In fact the rules are simple. Pace yourself, sip rather than swallow, and keep your glass full to avoid replenishment.

Vodka and toasts go together. Etiquette demands that it is the host who proposes the first toast. The Russian for "Cheers" is "*Na zdorovye.*"

Always toast your host and hostess separately.

If you have been invited round for a meal, and not for a special occasion, you may find yourself eating in the kitchen. Don't take this amiss. Far from indicating lack of regard, it is a compliment. In Russia, only close friends are received in the kitchen. In many families it is considered the coziest place and it is certainly the best loved.

More often than not, an evening in a Russian home consists of sitting at length round the table. The *hors d'oeuvres* are followed by the soup, the second course by tea and sweets, accompanied by different sorts of drink—for the men vodka, for the women, wine. It is quite normal to serve brandy with tea. The favorite entertainment during a meal for Russians is, first and foremost, conversation. They like telling anecdotes and, in an informal atmosphere, they will often sing. And all this, sitting round the table!

RECIPROCATION

Immediate reciprocation of the hospitality you have been shown is not expected of you. For your Russian partners you are a visitor to their country, which means that it is their job to receive and entertain you. If, in the future, they should visit your country, then they will expect the same sort of reception as they organized for you. However, if you would like to make a reciprocal gesture, you can invite your hosts to a restaurant. But be careful to choose the right restaurant. In Moscow, particularly, restaurants are socially differentiated. Your choice of restaurant says a lot about you. Consult your acquaintances, partners, or even the hotel staff. In Russia formality is not appreciated, so it may be better to postpone your return hospitality rather than respond in a formal way.

Meetings outside the office, meals, and receptions are an important component of business life in Russia. Your behavior in these social contexts is crucial to the establishment of good relations with your Russian partners. Don't forget that the main issues are not always decided in the office. Often this happens at an informal get-together, round a table. Have a serious attitude to such events, arm yourself with patience or, even better, enjoy yourself. It is not difficult!

chapter five

AT HOME

THE RUSSIAN FAMILY

Family and children are important in Russian life, although economic and social difficulties have drastically increased the divorce rate. One-child families are the norm and there is considerable admiration for parents with two or three children.

Because of the shortage of accommodation, it used to be common for young people to live with their parents, but today it is easier for young couples to set up home on their own. Seventy-five percent of Russians are apartment dwellers, and about 50 percent of homes are privately owned. In Soviet times all housing was state owned. By 1991 most housing had been privatized, making it possible to buy an apartment. Mortgages are now becoming more widely available and there is a huge amount of new property development taking place.

THE RESIDENCE PERMIT

Until recently all Russians had to have a residence permit, or *propiska*, stamped in their internal passports, authorizing them to live in a particular town. One would often see police checking permits in the street. The regulations governing residential registration for Russians are now being eased, but although the *propiska* was officially abolished in 1991, many local authorities still demand one. At the same time, the rules for noncitizens are getting stricter, in order to stop immigration from the former Soviet states.

DACHAS

The Russians love the countryside with an almost mystical reverence. Therefore, for a Russian to have a small cottage outside the city is a priority. It's called a *dacha*. Some *dachas* are mansions, others little more than shacks with a plot of land. They may not have running water or electricity, and that, too, is important in satisfying the "back to nature" longing of many Russians. The *dacha* is where the Russians feel most themselves, and to

be invited to one is a sign of personal confidence in you and an honor. The *dacha* is also an important source of fresh food. Most will have an allotment where the owners lovingly grow vegetables or fruit to be bottled and stored for use in the winter. On Friday afternoons offices empty early as people begin to leave the big cities for their *dachas* in the surrounding countryside.

CARS

In the big cities car-ownership is now much more common, as both Russian and imported cars become more available. It can be difficult finding somewhere to park, and driving conditions can be dangerous (See Chapter 7, Getting Around).

WORK

Most Russians will get up early and leave for work to arrive at their offices at 9:00 a.m. They will take an hour for lunch around 1:00 p.m. and then work through until 6:00 p.m. Working on Saturday is unusual in offices.

EVERYDAY SHOPPING

The Russians generally don't make a weekly trip to the supermarket, but shop when they need to.

In part this is a response to the psychology of shortage. If something became available in a shop, you immediately dropped everything and stood in line to buy it.

The Russians used to, and still do, carry a plastic bag with them for much of the time, to hold purchases.

In the past this was to take advantage of an opportunity. Today it's because Russian stores don't usually supply grocery bags. Where the "buy it immediately" psychology still exists is in the fashion stores. "If you see a Versace top, buy it. It may not be there tomorrow!"

Food shops are normally open Monday to Saturday from 8:00 a.m. to 1:00 p.m. and from 2:00 p.m. to 9:00 p.m; on Sundays from 8:00 a.m. to 1:00 p.m. Other shops open from 11:00 a.m. to 2:00 p.m. and from 3:00 p.m. to 9:00 p.m. Big stores such as GUM in Moscow are open all day. Outdoor markets (*rynok*) are good for fresh fruit and vegetables; most Russians buy their food in grocery stores or markets, which are felt to be better value for money than supermarkets. There are good-quality Western-style supermarkets in the big cities, which are popular with foreigners.

ECONOMIC LIFE

The Soviet Union aimed to provide a common measure of security. Every Russian was assured of an education, employment, access to healthcare, and a sense of belonging to the wider community.

Today life is much more insecure and the *bomzhi* (homeless people) and Russia's pensioners are the great losers. Russians have an ingrained respect for the elderly that is lacking in the West, and are prepared to spend more looking after old people in the family, but for those on their own there is no longer a safety net.

After 1991 food subsidies were removed, resulting in huge price rises in basic foodstuffs. By the end of 1999 annual inflation had jumped from 11 to 80 percent. In addition to this, the Russians have seen their savings wiped out, not once but twice, by the collapse of the banking system in 1993 and 1998. It is common for salaries to be paid in arrears (up to a year in some cases) and for debts to be defaulted on.

How do the Russians cope with economic downturns? By cutting down on imported luxuries such as coffee and wine, but still spending the same amount on children, leisure activities, and vodka. Despite relatively low annual incomes, in recent years the cash economy has been able to continue fueling a consumer boom.

Standards of Living

There are at least two types of urban Russian today. First there is a minority who are able to *remont*—"restore" a European standard of living, with a nice apartment, a car, and holidays abroad. The majority get by with difficulty. The average wage is $100 a month and pensioners receive $50 a month. About 44 million people in Russia live below the official poverty line of $32 a month.

Many Russians grow their own food on allotments or at their *dachas* outside the cities, and live on it throughout the winter. Those who are employed may be paid in products in lieu of wages, which they then barter for food. The result is a false "get by" economy in which there is little capital or taxes to pay for investment or services.

The New Russians

One economic group in Russia is doing very well—the new commercial elite who made fortunes out of buying the old state utilities. Called the "New Russians," they are equivalent to the American and British yuppies of the 1980s, and the butt of many Russian jokes.

Here's a typical one. New Russian 1: "Look at this Hermès tie. I got it for $200 in this store." New Russian 2: "Stupid! You could have got it for $400 round the corner."

Banking and Payments

Credit cards have been successfully introduced in larger cities, department stores, and supermarkets. However, after the crisis of fall 1998 they are no longer fully reliable. Therefore a certain amount of ready cash is highly recommended for your trip to Russia. The most widespread foreign currency is undoubtedly the American dollar. The Euro is still too new to be acceptable. It therefore makes sense in the short term to keep your money in dollars. That, after all, is what the Russians do.

All over cities like Moscow you will see currency-exchange kiosks. They are not for foreigners but for Russians. When ordinary Russians receive their salaries in rubles, they calculate what they will need for the month and then change the balance into dollars. Those dollars will be hidden away and will not find their way to a bank. The Russians have learned some hard lessons in the last ten years, and one of them is that banks cannot be trusted. Other kinds of hard currency, including British pounds, are exchanged rarely and reluctantly.

A word about the condition of your dollars. Only new, clean—ideally in mint condition—dollars are accepted for exchange. Even if they are only written on, they may be refused. In some banks, notes printed before 1990 have been refused. Russia's banking system is still radically different from the West's, especially as far as personal accounts are concerned. Money for a Russian means, first and foremost, cash. Personal accounts are considered to be unreliable, especially in a crisis, and are regarded only as a place in which to keep cash temporarily.

Prices
Prices in Russia are very unstable. Generally everything is quite expensive; Moscow is sometimes called the most expensive capital in Europe. On the other hand, some Russian products are still sold by "old" Communist-era prices which, when converted into dollars, cost next to nothing.

In Russia accommodation costs for foreigners remain low compared to the U.S.A. or the U.K. It is useful to know that the cost of accommodation in this country includes hot and cold water supply, heating, gas, and local (within the city) telephone calls. Electricity and long-distance calls are paid separately. The latter are very expensive.

EDUCATION
One of the great achievements of the Soviet Union was to take an overwhelmingly illiterate agrarian population and achieve 98 percent

literacy. A key educational aim of the Russian Federation is to uphold this achievement. The Soviet Union made schooling compulsory for at least eight years; now it is compulsory for nine years. To continue with school after the statutory graduation involves passing rigorous academic tests. The same applies for university entrance.

Russian education stresses reading and mathematics. Technical subjects such as science and mathematics are highly valued, and bright students are still encouraged to specialize from an early age. This has been criticized within Russia for limiting a child's educational choice, but nothing yet has changed.

Attitudes To Children

The Russians are crazy about children and are solicitous about their care and upbringing. Many foreigners have been surprised and offended by, usually, older Russian women approaching them in the street with advice on how to keep their young one's feet dry or head covered against the cold, or perhaps berating them because the child is too loud or too boisterous. Russian grandparents are free with their opinions and volunteer them robustly and without hesitation. If they do so, it's a reflection of care for the child rather than a criticism of you as a parent.

Russian teachers are well trained and are held in high regard socially. They are also government employees and therefore among the worst paid workers with the greatest arrears in salaries.

MILITARY SERVICE

At the age of eighteen, unless service is deferred for higher education, young men enroll for two to three years of military service. All conscripts have horror stories to tell about this. Basic training and boot camp are memorable experiences everywhere, and Russia is no exception. The regime is strict and often brutal, but gets less so as you progress and, presumably, as you become more senior, you can mete it out to others.

Exemption is hard to get, but one way is to be certified an "idiot," that is, as mentally or physically disabled. There are three classes of mental handicap. Classes 1 and 2 are to be avoided as they could get you incarcerated in a hospital or mental institution. But Class 3 leaves you free and able to benefit from certain concessions, food tickets, free transport, etc. A Russian joke has it that there are no idiots in the Russian army—below the rank of general!

chapter six

TIME OUT

The planning of one's free time in Russia is always difficult: there is so much to see and do. Take Moscow, for example. It is actually a collection of towns, in which one can find remnants of the old pre-Revolutionary Russia and super modernity, intellectual life of a very high order and the wildest sorts of entertainment. In a word, there is something for everyone.

When in Moscow don't change money on the streets, even if the exchange rate is favorable, as the chances of being cheated are very great. Do this at hotels, banks, and official exchange offices. Be careful altogether on the streets, particularly about buying foodstuffs and alcohol. It is safer to buy these more expensively in the big stores.

In Moscow and other big cities public toilets are virtually nonexistent. Toilets in restaurants, cafés, museums, theaters, and other public places are for customers or visitors to these venues only.

Don't always believe public signs. A "no smoking" sign, we have seen, does not necessarily apply, while "open round the clock" is by no means a guarantee that the doors will be open at any time of the day or night. It is best to check, so as not to find yourself in a tricky situation.

What do the Russians do in their free time? We have already seen that the *dacha* is the alternative center of Russian life, the place where people go when the weather is bearable. Another sanctuary is the *banya*—especially in the regions.

THE *BANYA*

The *banya,* or bathhouse, occupies a prominent place in Russian life. In the provinces and villages it is still the main means of keeping oneself clean, while in the major cities it is regarded as a pastime that is both enjoyable and good for your health. For many Russians it is a pleasure they would not dream of giving up. The *banya* is the equivalent of the Finnish sauna (which is becoming popular in Russia), but differs from it in that it has a stone stove. A visit to one of the old Moscow bathhouses such as the Sanduny Baths (Neglinnaya Street, 14) is an interesting cultural experience.

The *banya* is a place for meeting and relaxing. You go in, pay a modest fee, change, and go through your ablutions before emerging into the high temperatures of the stone stove room. When you've had enough, you go into the steam room, where you can whip yourself with a switch of dried birch leaves, after which you immerse yourself in the cold bath (in the countryside in winter hardy souls plunge into a snowdrift). Later, cleansed and refreshed, you can enjoy a drink before reemerging into the world.

If you are invited to the *banya,* don't take it as a hint that it is time you had a wash, but as your host's wish to give you pleasure. To be invited to the *banya* by a business colleague is an honor and a sign of confidence. It is also a confirmation that your business is going well.

MUSEUMS

Russia has wonderful museums. Moscow is the cultural center of Russia and the chance to visit its main museums should not be missed. Here you can become acquainted with Russian icons, the various Russian art movements, and modern art. There are fine collections of Western European art, and opportunities to learn about Russian history and the life and work of Russia's leading writers, scientists, and other outstanding individuals. One unmissable museum is the Tretyakov Gallery (Lavrushinsky Street, 12), with its collections of Russian icons, paintings, and Soviet art. Lovers of the French Impressionists and Post-Impressionists should visit the Pushkin Fine Art Museum

(Volkhonka Street), which has one of the best collections of French art of this period in the world. In St. Petersburg, of course, there is the world-famous Hermitage Museum. Housed in the beautiful green-and-white Winter Palace, this is one of the world's great art collections, with almost three million exhibits.

THEATER AND CONCERTS

In the Soviet era, before *perestroika*, the role of theater in the cultural and spiritual life of the Russian people was enormous, and this is now returning. While in order to appreciate Russian drama some knowledge of the language is necessary, ballet and opera are accessible to everyone, and a visit to the Bolshoi Theater in Moscow or the Kirov Ballet and Opera at the Mariinsky Theater in St. Petersburg is almost a pilgrimage for music lovers. It is *de rigueur* to dress formally for concerts.

CINEMA

In the last ten years, the cinema has lost its role as the "entertainer" of the Russian masses. The majority of cinemas are now privately owned. In Moscow, St. Petersburg, and many big cities new fashionable cinemas of the Western type have appeared. In some, for instance, the American House of Cinema at the Radisson-Slavyanskaya Hotel and The Cinema under the Dome at the Olympic Penta Hotel, you can watch films in English. Most films are dubbed into Russian.

MARKETS

Street markets play an important role in the capital's life. The most popular (and expensive) produce market with foreigners is the Cheremushkinsky Market in Moscow, where you can buy anything from meat to whatever berries are in season. There are markets of this sort in every big Russian town. Do not mistake these, however, for the flea markets where you can buy cheap goods, or the wholesale markets where you can buy goods from all over the world and foodstuffs cheaper than in the shops, although there is no guarantee of quality. The wholesale markets are a fairly new phenomenon and have become very popular. Traditional markets sell only agricultural produce that is mainly grown or produced by the seller.

Foreigners in Moscow tend to flock to Arbat Street. Here you will find old buildings, numerous shops, street traders selling souvenirs, buskers, and artists. The Arbat, which is a pedestrian precinct, is always noisy and full of people.

SHOPPING

Russian shops stock a mixture of Western brand
names and cheap goods from the Far East. In
Moscow there are also exclusive Western
boutiques. What they have in common is the
Russian style of trading, which means bargaining
for everything. For visitors, the best purchases are
traditional Russian souvenirs. Beware the many
fakes on sale: the genuine article always has a
trademark and often the name of the artist who
made it underneath. It is important to realize that
the relatively high price of some souvenirs reflects
the fact that they are works of art. The wooden
egg cup with the traditional design you buy may
well have been hand-turned, not mass produced,
and decorated by hand, not with a transfer. The
matryoshka wooden dolls are always popular.

There are many unique Russian folk arts and
crafts. Among them are the exquisite lacquered
miniature boxes made in the villages of Palekh,
Mstiora, and Fedoskino. Scenes from traditional
Russian fairy tales and legends, as well as
historical and literary characters, are painted on
these in glowing colors on a black-laquered
background. Generally, the smaller the box, the
more valuable and expensive it is.

One of the most sought-after delicacies, for
Russians and visitors alike, is caviar. The most
expensive is black caviar from the eggs of the

sturgeon; somewhat cheaper is red caviar, from salmon; and cheapest of all is the pink whitefish caviar. The traditional source of caviar is the Caspian Sea, but pollution in recent years has increased the rarity of the product and raised prices. Caviar should be sealed in jars, tightly packed with complete, unbroken eggs, and should smell of fresh fish. It should never be more than six months old. Check the packaging and dates.

The best-quality vodka is obtainable in leading Moscow and St. Petersburg shops. Russian furs are very good value. Other worthwhile purchases are good-quality art books, particularly on Russian art, and music recordings, classical as well as Russian folk instrumental. Gold and silver jewelry, especially semiprecious stones from the Urals, is very good value. As a general rule, in Moscow and other Russian towns it is best to buy items that have been made locally. The closer you are to the place of manufacture, the lower the price.

THE KREMLIN AND LENIN'S TOMB

Moscow has an almost mystical significance as the heart of the nation, and it is an ideal of all Russians to visit it one day. If Moscow is the heart of Russia, then the Kremlin compound is, without doubt, the heart of Moscow. According to the ancient Russian Chronicle, in 1147 Grand Prince

Yuri Dolgoruki, the founder of Moscow, "gave a most sumptuous banquet." This is regarded as the founding date of the city. The first settlement was on the site of the present-day Kremlin where, by 1156, wooden walls had been erected. The walls that we see today were built later—in the fifteenth to seventeenth centuries—by Italian master craftsmen who were working in Russia.

The most important sights in the Kremlin for both Russian and foreign visitors are the Cathedral of the Assumption (1479), where the Tsars were crowned and the Metropolitans and Patriarchs of the Russian Orthodox Church were buried, and the Armory Palace and the Diamond Fund collections. Also in the Kremlin is the Palace of Congresses, which was built in 1961 as a venue for Communist Party congresses. Today it is used for concerts and ballet performances.

Russian visitors next visit Red Square (*Krasnaya Ploshchad*), which adjoins the Kremlin. The most striking sight in the square is St. Basil's Cathedral, built in 1555–60 to commemorate Ivan the Terrible's conquest of Kazan. According to legend, Ivan was so enchanted with the result that he had the architects blinded so that they might never again create a church of such magnificence.

Another famous sight on Red Square is the
Lenin Mausoleum. Not so long ago a place of
mass pilgrimage, the mausoleum today is the
subject of lively debate: should Lenin's embalmed
body remain where it is, or should the leader of
the world proletariat be buried according to
Russian Orthodox tradition. Leading public
figures of the Soviet era are buried behind the
mausoleum in (or by) the Kremlin wall.

In the last few years there has been an effort to
restore the exteriors of old buildings to their
former glory, while gutting and modernizing the
insides. This is particularly noticeable on St.
Petersburg's glorious Nevsky Prospekt, one of
Europe's most distinguished streets.

OPEN SPACES

If you're stuck in the city,
try a park. The favorite
park in Moscow for
foreigners is Gorky Park,
made famous in the novel by Martin Cruz Smith.
Muscovites, however, recommend Sokolniki Park
or the Alexander Gardens, running along the
Kremlin walls on the northwest side.

From the Sparrow Hills (until recently the
Lenin Hills) on the outskirts of Moscow there is
an unforgettable panoramic view of the city.

THE COUNTRYSIDE

Invitations to go on trips to the countryside are very common, especially in the summer—to *dachas*, on excursions, or simply to get out of the city. From the Caucasians the Russians have borrowed the tradition of *shashliks*, or barbecues —grilling meat, fish, chicken, or vegetables over hot charcoal in the open air. Trips to the countryside are considered one of the best ways of entertaining and establishing contact with one's foreign partners.

THE MOSCOW METRO

Moscow's famous subway is a sight in its own right, and excursions on the Metro are very popular with visitors. Although in recent years it has become somewhat less spick and span, its marble, mosaics, plasterwork, sculptures, and original designs continue to delight the eye. The first line, built in 1935, linked the stations of Sokolniki and Park Kultury. The most impressive stations are Ploschad Revoluzi'i, Teatralnaya, Mayakovskaya, Kievskaya, and Komsomolskaya. The morning rush hour on the Metro lasts until about 10:00 a.m., and the evening rush hour starts after 4:00 p.m. It is best to avoid using the Metro at these times—it is not a cultural experience that can be recommended to visitors.

CULTURAL PROGRAMS

Apart from business lunches and suppers, the Russians like to organize what they refer to as "cultural programs." These may include outings to the theater or ballet. The Russians enjoy dressing up for the theater: it is considered a special occasion. Foreigners are also often taken to the circus. Don't consider this to be a comment on your intellectual capacity. The Russian circus is one of the best in the world and the Russians are right to be proud of it. It is a colorful spectacle that you will almost certainly enjoy.

FUN

Big city life can be fun. Moscow has become the new "rave" center for jet-setting clubbers and St. Petersburg's "White Nights," the season in summer when the sun never sets, is famous for its parties and all-night street entertaining.

At a less salubrious level, foreigners are used to being called in their hotels to be asked if they would like to meet "a nice Russian lady." Just say "No," and you won't be bothered. Should you say "Yes," be careful when you open your hotel room door that only the nice Russian lady comes in, and that she is not followed by a nice Russian gentleman with intent to rob!

SPORT

One of the ways the old Soviet Union made its mark in the outside world was in the success of its sporting heroes, especially in athletics (particularly gymnastics) and in track-and-field events. Indeed, in 1980 Moscow hosted the summer Olympic Games. Moscow's Dynamo football team and its ice hockey and other winter sports teams have also had considerable success internationally. One of the difficulties facing athletes and sporting organizations in the new Russia is that, under pressure of economic reform, the huge funds formerly allocated to sport, as a way of gaining international publicity, have largely dried up.

On the other hand, for visitors to Russia today, new sporting opportunities present themselves in hunting and fishing safaris. Since so many areas have been closed to the outside world for so many years, game abounds and, although there is a problem with illegal fishing and hunting, many reputable agencies now offer sponsored trips.

Russia also has a number of great mountain ranges, some of which are barely known in the West. The Caucasus, Altai, Sayan, and Stanovoy mountains all offer mountain climbing opportunities, as do some of the peaks along the Kamchatka peninsula. Alpine skiing facilities exist, but are still somewhat limited.

EATING AND DRINKING

In recent years, a large number of Western-style restaurants have opened in the major cities and your Russian hosts will entertain you there, for appearances' sake. However, if given the choice of deciding where to dine, it's probably best to go for traditional rather than international restaurants. Regional cuisine is widely represented in Moscow and St. Petersburg, especially Georgian and Armenian cooking, and Georgian wine. Of course, these restaurants will be stylized, far from authentic, and more likely than not geared to the entertainment of foreigners. The menus may be in Russian and English or in Russian and German. You may find yourself feeling somewhat lost in such places, and it is best to go with a Russian.

It is not usual to split the bill. Generally an invitation to a restaurant means that all expenses are taken care of, unless otherwise agreed at the outset. The important thing is not to pay your share, but to reciprocate the invitation. For a Russian, going to a restaurant is considered a special occasion, a social outing. In a cafeteria, on the other hand, you should offer to pay for yourself as a courtesy. You probably won't be alowed to.

If, as a businesswoman, you find yourself in a male collective, it will be rare for you to pay for yourself. Even if the invitation originates from you, the men, particularly the older generation, will probably not allow you to pay and, if you insist, they may take it as a personal slight. In such a situation, you might try saying that it is your firm that is paying the bill and not you personally, though even this will not always be understood by the Russians. The situation will be different if you are in female company, or that of young people.

Restaurants can be expensive and should be booked in advance. Hours are usually noon to 3:00 p.m. for lunch and 7:00 p.m. till 11:00 p.m. for dinner. In some restaurants at lunchtime you may have to share a table with strangers.

Russian restaurants used to be famous for the surliness of their staff—waiters who would make you wait hours before taking your order and then virtually throw the food at you when serving it. These people still exist, but the service culture is growing fast, especially in the new international restaurants in the big cities.

Be prepared to have your space violated in a restaurant. The tables may be quite close together, and a Russian who has drunk too much is no respecter of personal space as he tries to weave his way out of the room. Keep a sense of humor and try to enjoy the experience if it occurs.

chapter seven

GETTING AROUND

Russian customs and immigration officials can be less than friendly, particularly to other races or to minority groups such as gays. To avoid problems, make sure your paperwork is in order.

There are three kinds of visa—tourist, business, and private. Formally you should have a letter of invitation to Russia: this may be provided by your

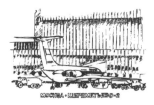

tour company, your business partner, or even by Russian Embassy or Consular officials. You may be asked to provide a similar letter for Russians visiting you.

Officially you should register within three days of arrival with the local foreign police (OVIR). This is a simple formality and usually your hotel or the office you are visiting will do it for you. When you leave the country your visa may be removed and your residence checked. Save your tickets to prove where you have been.

Nowadays it's easy to apply for a visa over the Internet. A number of services are available, but

the simplest is to log on to www.visatorussia.com.
The standard time for issuing a visa is ten working
days. You cannot obtain a visa at the airport on
arrival. Tourist visas are single- or double-entry
and are issued for no longer than thirty days.
Single- and double-entry business visas are issued
for up to ninety days, and multiple reentry visas
for up to one year can be obtained from the
Russian Ministry of Foreign Affairs. Private visas
are issued for single-entry only, up to ninety days.

TO ENTER RUSSIA YOU NEED
- An invitation
- Money and goods-imported declaration
  (including things like wedding rings)
- Passport
- Visa

TO LEAVE RUSSIA YOU NEED
- Passport
- Visa
- Declaration of what you are taking out
  (form given to you on entry, unless you
  went through the green channel)

In theory, the Russian state needs to know
where you will be staying every night of your visit.
Many people do not bother to register this

information, but if you don't do so problems may arise when you want to leave the country, or when you want to return, perhaps after a short trip abroad. So it is worth making sure that your documentation and your visa status are in order.

Carry your passport and residence documents around with you always. They might be requested by the police at any time. For security, you should make photocopies of all documents.

Because visitors are required by law to include every town and village they intend to visit on their visa, the police can deport them if they are found in the wrong place without permission.

If, when challenged by the police, you are asked to sign a protocol, you must refuse. If you sign it, it is basically an admission of guilt and your embassy can't help you. If you are asked to surrender your passport, once again it is important to refuse. Remember, too, that in the autonomous republics the local constitution may carry more weight than in Moscow. Not every state insists that all the cities you visit be listed in your visa, but many do.

HOTELS

In Moscow and St. Petersburg the top-class Western-style hotels are identical to their equivalents in the U.S.A. and Europe. They may be a little more expensive. The Balchug-Kempinski and the Radisson-Slavianskaya, for example, are five-star hotels with prices to match. At the other extreme, there are very cheap hotels of such low standards that they are likely to cause culture shock! If you are very short of money and staying in a twenty-dollar room (the minimum hotel price in Moscow), be prepared for cockroaches, dirt, cracked glasses, a broken table, a drunken neighbor next door, a bathroom in the corridor, and no hint of comfort. In Moscow and St. Petersburg such hotels are only among the cheapest; in some provincial towns there may be nothing else.

Choose your hotel on the recommendation of someone you know who has stayed there, or on the advice of your Russian partners. Try to book it through them, specifying your requirements beforehand. Remember that in Russia price does not always correspond to quality—Russian hotels are usually more expensive than in the U.S.A. and Europe and standards are lower. Don't be surprised by a broken handle or a leaking tap. The reason for this is not carelessness, but lack of cash. It is not necessary to provide your own bathplug and toilet paper in Moscow or St. Petersburg, but it may be in other cities.

Certain aspects of the strict Soviet hotel regime are still alive, especially in the provinces. When checking in, your passport will be requested and, sometimes, payment in advance. Sharing a room with a person of the opposite sex whose name differs from yours may cause problems. Although night inspections by the militia checking on your "moral behavior" are a thing of the past, some elderly *babushka* on duty, who approves only of legally registered marriages, might ask questions.

On registering you are given a "guest card," which is your official pass to the hotel. Keep it with you. The idea behind it is to protect your security and to limit the admittance of thieves, prostitutes, and black marketeers into the hotel.

Remember that not all people working in a hotel can speak foreign languages, and it is worth learning a few useful Russian phrases. Generally though, there will be somebody around who knows a little English and will be eager to help.

The *Dezhurnaya*

Presiding over each floor of the larger and older hotels is the floor manager, or *dezhurnaya*. This lady is responsible for the rooms on her floor. She requires special handling. If you are on good terms with her she will provide you with every comfort, but don't expect prompt service. She may be absent when you need her, having tea with a colleague, or talking on the phone. This kind of "independent" behavior on the part of service people can be seen as a way of compensating for their lowly position. Their wages are low, but they can't be dismissed because it is difficult to find staff for low-paid work. Some are university graduates who have taken on this humble job in unfortunate circumstances. A poem from the Soviet era by the poet and playwright Vladimir Mayakovsky sums it up: "Soviet people have their own pride: we look down on the bourgeoisie."

To get cooperation, a small sign of attention or respect, or a little souvenir, can help melt the ice. If you speak a little Russian, take time to talk to her. Complaining about something can be a great help. Pity and sympathy are Russian qualities and the positive result may surprise you.

Barflies

The presence of refugees from former Soviet republics can be a problem in Moscow hotel bars and lobbies. They may not lack money but, being uprooted, they often have social problems and may be dangerous. The best way to behave if approached is not to pay any attention to them.

Don't Expect Too Much

We have seen that the average Rusian hotel lacks the comfort and convenience of its equivalent elsewhere. Apart from the economic difficulties, the Russian idea of comfort differs from that of the West. If the room is warm, dry, and clean, a Russian traveler will be happy. Before getting angry at, say, having no hot water, try to understand the situation. For instance, in summer in Moscow the city's central heating system is always switched off for a month, and no amount of fuss can change it. (Only the largest hotels have their own generators and hot water supplies.)

Room service in the average provincial hotel is usually confined to providing you with boiling water, or sometimes a kettle. Ironing can be a problem, so take a travel iron. In most Moscow hotels washing clothes by yourself is out of the question, yet laundry can take a week to come back. The food in such hotels is also variable. If you prefer convenience to price and quality you can eat there, otherwise go downtown. In small provincial towns, however, the hotel restaurant is often the best there is.

Drinking tap water in the hotel is not recommended. Bottled mineral water is available. If you do swallow ordinary tap water, don't panic. Water-borne disease is rare in Russia.

On leaving the hotel you may have to "return" your room to a chambermaid. This system is falling into disuse, but there are still places where the chambermaid will thoroughly check every glass, used towel, and the linen. This procedure may seem strange and humiliating to you, but it is a time-honored practice. The wage of the woman on duty is very low. This explains why she is so particular about checking every object—she will have to pay for anything that is missing.

APARTMENTS

If you are staying in one place for a month or more, renting an apartment is a good idea—apartments are cheaper, more convenient, and give you more freedom. It is not customary in Russia to invite people to a hotel room, so an apartment enables you to meet both business partners and friends more easily.

TAXIS

Taxis are best summoned by telephone. It is a little more expensive than hailing them, and may take longer, but it is safer. Nowadays in Moscow there are many private cab companies; you can find their telephone numbers in the directory or ask at the hotel reception desk.

Normally you'll use a city-registered cab service, whether booked directly or through the hotel. Neither the operators nor the drivers are likely to speak English, however. Get someone to write your destination down in Russian on a piece of paper and show it to the driver. In a city like Moscow, the official taxis are yellow with a black-and-white check design on the roof and on the door. Taxis for hire may or may not display a green light. Always agree on the fare before you start your journey.

The Russians hail taxis in the street. They also pay for lifts in private cars. For many Russian car owners this is an easy way to get quick cash. It's easier to find a *chastnik* (the owner of a private car) than a taxi, and it may be as much as three times cheaper. Some drivers only take passengers going in their direction, so don't be disappointed or hurt if they refuse to give you a lift: it has nothing to do with you, only with your route. Agree on the price before the trip. Once a packet of foreign cigarettes was enough to cover Moscow from end to end. That is no longer true. Cash in rubles is more acceptable than foreign currency.

CAR RENTAL

Renting a car in the big cities is easy now that foreign car-rental companies have opened offices in Russia. Fuel is always leaded. A98 (superplus) and A95 (super) are recommended for foreign cars. But driving a car in Russia can be difficult.

Bad traffic jams and occasional gasoline shortages should make you think twice before renting a car. However, people who are used to driving in Naples, or sitting in traffic jams in London or New York, are convinced that driving in the big cities of Russia is no worse than in the West.

Do I Need A Car?

Driving in Russia's major cities is not easy. Traffic discipline is not good and the roads are often in poor condition. Russian drivers can be aggressive and inconsiderate about giving way. Although the road signs follow international conventions, the writing is in Cyrillic. And there is the weather. At the very least, you will need studded tires in winter (November to April, and even May). Parking in the center of cities like Moscow is expensive. There are parking attendants who will fix things for you, but no parking meters. In Moscow you pay when you arrive or leave and periods are measured in half hours. Police fines can be high for parking in restricted areas.

The key problem for motorists is the traffic police (GIBDD—*Gosudarstvennaya Inspektsiya Bezopasnosti Dorozhnogo Dvizheniya*), who have the power to impose on-the-spot fines. They can stop you at any time and ask for documents. Not having a first-aid kit or a fire extinguisher is a good reason for a fine, as is driving without all seatbelts fastened if you have passengers. Most fines are the equivalent of five or ten dollars. It is best simply to pay up, as the fines are a recognized way for the police to supplement their low incomes.

If you are staying in Russia for any length of time, and live in the suburbs or outside the city, then a car is probably a good idea. But make sure you have a parking space at either end of your most regular journeys. Many Russians leave their cars under the snow when winter arrives, taking out the batteries and returning when the snow thaws.

Cars are valuable and a new or clean and unmarked foreign car is a magnet both for itself and what's inside it. Don't leave valuables and car radios in view, and make sure your car is properly locked and protected.

If you're driving between cities, rely on a good map rather than on signposts, as smaller villages en route may be poorly marked.

SUBWAYS

The underground railway network system is efficient. The Moscow Metro has ten lines covering the city, all color-coded. Everything used to be in Cyrillic. Today some stations, and many trains, use English transliteration as well. Should you be faced with Cyrillic signs only, learn to recognize the spelling of your destination and

count the stations back to your starting point.
This should allow you to get off where you need
to. Metro stations are well staffed, but, of course,
by Russian speakers. Fares are standard for all
journeys and tickets are cheap.

Like most underground systems, it is possible
to buy a monthly pass or a
magnetic card, allowing
twenty or sixty rides. As
you go through the
barrier, the card flashes
up how many rides you
have left. It is always
worth buying a multiple-ride
card as lines for tickets can mean long delays,
especially in the morning and evening. Buy your
cards from the *Kassa* (ticket office) in the Metro
station. Children under six travel free of charge.

BUSES
These may be Eastern European-style tramcars,
trolleybuses, or regular buses. Many of them link
up with the Metro system.

The buses work on a punch-card system. You
can buy tickets at a Metro station, from a kiosk, or
from the driver. Punch your card when you board
the bus to validate your journey. On some routes
it is possible to buy tickets from the conductor.

TRAINS

Traveling by train in Russia is a communal experience. Distances are long and space can be tight. It is normal to greet your fellow passengers on entering your compartment. It is normal to talk, to share cigarettes, candies, or even drinks. Never play cards for money, however—there are many professional card sharks, called "*katala.*"

The biggest adaptation may be in the sleeping arrangements. Your compartment may have four berths, which you will share with complete strangers. After talking for a while, everybody will turn in and sleep until the train arrives at the destination. At the end of the carriage there may be an attendant with a samovar, serving tea. Long journeys such as this have given rise to many a traveler's tale.

Russian Black Humor

In Soviet times, a passenger, wishing to play a joke on his fellow travelers, told the samovar attendant to bring tea for everybody in the compartment exactly twenty minutes after the train left the station. After eighteen minutes, as the passengers were chatting, he said, "Comrade Stalin knows everything, even what we are talking about right here." Everyone disagreed volubly, but he continued, "The KGB hears everything. If I said 'KGB, bring us tea right now,' it would appear." As everyone laughed at him, the door opened and the attendant appeared with four cups of tea. Surprise and amusement kept the conversation and the vodka flowing longer than usual.

The following morning, in the sleepy light of dawn, the passenger awoke and stumbled out to the toilet. He returned and opened the door to find the compartment empty. Horrified, he ran down the carriage, and found the attendant.

"The comrades in Compartment J, they've gone!" he shouted. "I know," said the attendant, "the KGB came in and arrested them." "But why?" asked the distraught passenger. "Apparently they were laughing at Comrade Stalin," he replied. "But it was my fault," wailed the passenger, "Why didn't the KGB arrest me as well?" "The Comrade Major enjoyed your joke," came the reply.

WALKING

Map distances can be misleading. Crossing a couple of squares and going one block may actually involve a long walk: large Russian cities are more American in scale than European.

Jaywalking is illegal in cities, but everybody does it. If you stand at a crossing waiting for the lights to change, everyone will assume you have paused, struck by a sudden thought or inspiration. However, if you are stopped by the police for crossing the road between authorized crossings, you will be charged a small on-the-spot fine (the equivalent of five or ten dollars).

It's worth noting that, although there are pedestrian crossings in cities, these are ignored by motorists, unless they have green lights signaling to pedestrians that they have the right of way.

And here's something you might not have thought about—manhole covers. This may sound like a Keystone Cops joke, but check as you walk across them. They don't always fit and may rock violently or even collapse as you step on them.

FINDING YOUR WAY

Until you know your way around, it is vital to carry your destination address written down in Russian. Then if you need to ask for help, you can show people the piece of paper. Opposite are the types of streets you will encounter, and their common abbreviations.

Remember that to find an apartment, two things are important—the number of the building and the number of the entrance. So if someone gives you directions to their apartment, they would say, for example, Stroenie L, Podezd 15 (Building L, Entrance 15).

English Name	Russian Name	Abbreviation
Avenue	*Prospekt*	Pr
Bridge	*Most*	
Building	*Stroenie*	Str
Cul-de-sac	*Tupik*	
Entrance	*Podezd*	pd
Garden/park	*Sad*	
Lane	*Pereulok*	Per
Passage	*Proezd*	Pr
Road	*Shosse*	Sh
Square	*Ploschad*	Pl
Street	*Ulitsa*	Ul

CLOTHES

Sturdy shoes are essential, and the sturdier the better. Shoes will be rotted by damp, by snow, by the salt put on the roads in January and February to melt the snow, and by the grit used to make the sidewalks less slippery.

In winter you will need warm coats and a hat with earflaps. Remember that when you go into a building it will be well heated, so wear things you can remove without embarrassment. Layered clothing is best.

HEALTH

Russian doctors are highly qualified and extremely knowledgeable. Nevertheless, the health infrastructure is uncertain, and it is advisable to take out medical insurance before departure offering the highest level of care. If you are on medication, bring enough with you to last your stay. If you are ill, go to your nearest American Medical Center or American Dental Center.

In following this advice you would not be doing anything a middle-class Russian would not do if he or she could.

Vaccinations

You should consider the following vaccinations before departure for Russia: Diphtheria, Tetanus, and Hepatitis A and B. If you are staying longer than three months, you are required to have a certificate stating that you have been tested to ensure that you are not HIV Positive.

SECURITY

Western visitors often arrive full of apprehension, having heard stories about the Russian Mafia, crime, and the free-for-all that reigns in the cities. Of course, if you compare the situation in Russia today to that of twenty years ago, there are many more infringements of law and order and there is less personal safety. If, however, you compare Moscow or St. Petersburg to any other major city in the world, the security situation is very similar.

The former Soviet Union was a highly militarized and security-conscious state. In the

Russian Federation much of that military training has now gone into private security. The Mafia, Russian style, is a reality and large numbers of Russian businessmen pay money to a *krysha* (Russian for "roof") for "protection." In spite of some high-profile gangland killings in the 1990s, this violence doesn't affect ordinary people.

Any densely populated city can be dangerous if you do not take the usual, common sense precautions. It is not wise to take chance acquaintances you meet on the street back to your hotel room, to wander about the city if you've had one too many, to wave large wads of money around, and so forth.

Many social problems that are new for Russians are sadly familiar to Western visitors, who are well used to ignoring homeless and unemployed people on the streets. It is important to go without negative feelings. In Russia there is a saying: "Whatever you are frightened of will happen to you."

Russia's cities have an excitement about them as people experience, and experiment with, new freedoms and opportunities, and face new challenges and difficulties.

Traveling in Russia can be an adventure. If you are on your own, you must be able to speak Russian. Failing that, it would be best, at least for the first time, to travel with a tourist group or with Russian speakers.

chapter eight

BUSINESS BRIEFING

THE RUSSIAN ECONOMY

Russia is one of the world's richest countries in raw materials, and most of that wealth lies east of the Ural Mountains in Siberia and in Russia's Far East. Siberia has a third of the world's gold reserves. Yakutia and Mirny are centers for diamond mining. The gold and diamond seams in Kolyma in the north of Siberia exceed those of South Africa. The oil and gas fields equal those of the Arabian Gulf. Russia's timber resources are greater than Brazil's.

These facts alone should make Russia one of the most significant, popular, and profitable targets of overseas investment and the source of riches for the Russian people. That the majority of Russians are still very poor needs an explanation, and the explanation is historical.

First, however, the good news. Since the oil discoveries of the 1960s, Gazprom, Russia's state-owned oil and gas company, is one of the country's biggest earners and a mainstay of the Russian economy. Largely due to oil and gas exports, Russia's economy has been growing at about 5 percent a year, despite its problems.

Siberia and Russia's Far East, with the exception of individual cities such as Vladivostock, are economically disadvantaged by comparison with Russia west of the Urals, and people are often bitterly angry at Moscow's monopoly on "their" local resources.

In 1991 the new pro-market Russian government moved rapidly to privatize the 180,000 state-owned businesses, much with local government investment or interest. By 1994 100,000 businesses had been sold off. After 1992 there was an 80 percent cut in military and defense spending. This caused strong conservative resistance, and also led to greater poverty in the "rustbelt" factory area, hitherto uneconomically sustained by the Soviet system. The short-term effects of privatization and deregulation, coupled with the collapse of the banking system in 1993 and 1998, were rampant inflation and the contraction of the economy.

In this context, the role of the International Monetary Fund, the E.U., Germany, and the U.S.A. has been crucial in supporting Russia with loans. In 1998 the failure of Russia's harvest meant that the U.S.A. and the E.U. were asked to provide over five million tons of food aid to Russia. This phase will pass as the new economic structures become more established in Russia, and the world economy recovers its nerve.

Economic trends in Russia in 2002 remained positive, although GDP was projected to decline slightly. The rate of inflation, 21.6 percent in 2001, was expected to go down to 15.7 percent for 2002, while unemployment was holding steady at just over 8 percent. The ruble had strengthened against the dollar, and the country was slowly beginning to pay off its enormous foreign debt, estimated at $154 billion at the end of 2001.

THE BUSINESS CULTURE

In today's Russia the Western term "businessman" has gained wide currency. The name covers a variety of types of businesspeople (usually men).

The "New Russians"

These are people who made their money during the ten years of Boris Yeltsin's government. One of their most distinguishing features is conspicuous consumption. The amount of money necessary to achieve this happy state varies according to social context. For some, the latest Mercedes, a private residence on the Rublyovskoe Highway (the most prestigious address in suburban Moscow), and a villa on the Mediterranean are a must. Others are content with a secondhand Opel, an apartment with Euro-standard interior décor, and a case of expensive good quality vodka to celebrate the holiday with. What they all have in common is the desire to flaunt their wealth.

In Russia, to begin with, the "New Russians" aroused irritation and jealousy: "There is nothing to eat, and they fling their money around. What have they done to deserve it?" Today, this attitude is changing to one of grudging acceptance ("Since he exists, he must be meant to be"), and even pity ("You had better enjoy life while you can, poor devil: for you'll end up bankrupt or even murdered"). Generally speaking, the Russians are patient and compassionate.

Westerners tend to refer to all Russian businessmen as "New Russians." In Russia itself this is a derogatory term reserved for those who want to get their hands on "easy" money and spend it as quickly as possible. The antics of the "New Russians" have given rise to countless quips illustrating their crass behavior.

The Intelligentsia
Among the "serious" Russian businessmen are members of the intelligentsia—graduates of the country's leading institutions of higher education,

often with several degrees and other academic titles. They have gone into business either to make money, or to enjoy the new opportunities open to them to develop their abilities. For foreigners contact with such people is, as a rule, quite straightforward. The Russian *intelligent* is fairly cosmopolitan in his views, well educated—be ready to chat to a former engineer with excellent knowledge of nineteenth-century American poetry and/or Italian Renaissance painting—speaks foreign languages, and knows the world, if only through literature, newspapers, the Voice of America, and Western films.

Acquaintance with a businessman-*intelligent*, even if you are not linked by common interests, will always be useful, since education in Russia today, though it does not bring in money, is rated extremely highly. Moreover, as a rule, an educated man has good contacts, is respected by those who surround him, including people in business circles, knows his way around, and can always advise on how to react to a given situation.

The Old Guard

The other large group of businessmen consists of the so-called "old guard." These are people who gained wide experience in administrative, Party, and organizational work in the Soviet period, who have adjusted to the post-Communist reality, and are now putting their abilities to good use in new spheres of activity. Such people tend to be hypercautious. They take their time in conducting negotiations, doing so with feeling, deriving pleasure from the process as from a game of chess, and it is often difficult for foreigners to foresee or gauge their thoughts and actions. They are very well connected and therefore have great potential, since "contacts," as always, play a major role in Russian life—though now, instead of being used to obtain a pair of French boots or tickets to the Bolshoi Ballet, they can help to start up a company, get around the law, or secure a contract.

This group will not deceive you in small things but may do so in large ones. Over the years they have developed a peculiar code of honor of their own: they are capable of large-scale intrigue, but will never take a risk in minor matters—"one has to think of one's reputation."

The Younger Generation
It is much easier to get along with the younger generation of Russian businessmen. These young people have no experience of working in the Soviet system. They are familiar with the Western way of conducting negotiations, are happy to acquire new habits, more likely to speak foreign languages than the old-timers, and dislike putting things off. With some of them you may feel as if

you are in the company of fellow countrymen!

However, it is here that one is most likely to run up against deceit and petty swindling. Beneath the veneer of Western efficiency there may lurk an irresponsible risk-taker who has only superficially absorbed Western business values and is not to be trusted. Be warned: quick wits and haste may conceal deception, while slowness may derive from caution, experience, and reluctance to take a risk.

It is also important to have a relaxed attitude about the political convictions of your business partners and to forget the usual labels. A man calling himself a Communist (and in particular the man who talks nostalgically of the good old days) may be a first-class businessman, a reliable partner, and highly intelligent—however much this combination of attributes may seem to contradict your own world view. In Russian politics today everything is very confused. For the duration of your business negotiations, therefore, put aside your preconceptions and convictions.

BUSINESS ETIQUETTE

Business etiquette in Russia today is still in the process of taking shape, basing itself partly on pre-Revolutionary, partly on Soviet, and partly on Western patterns. This explosive mixture— unstable, indeterminate, and not always pleasant—explains the behavior of the majority of Russian businessmen. One should constantly bear in mind that life in Russia, the business world included, is changing very rapidly. What appeared to be totally impossible ten years ago, the very concept of Russian business, for example, is today a feature of everyday life. Who knows what tomorrow will bring?

PREPARING FOR A VISIT

Careful preparation for a business trip to Russia is vital. An exchange of faxes and e-mails setting out the aims and goals of the trip is useful; don't count on the ordinary postal service, which is extremely unreliable in Russia. You will never find out at what stage your letters went astray.

Always take copies of correspondence with you to meetings. First, the people who correspond with you are not necessarily those who will be conducting the negotiations: it is possible you will have to spend time going over things you thought were already done. Secondly, don't write reams. Remember that for the recipients English is a foreign language and not all are completely fluent in it. List your main goals and formulate them as simply and clearly as possible. Finally, remember that in Russia there exists a peculiar attitude to the printed word and to any kind of official document or instruction. Whereas in the Western world an official document carries a lot of weight, in Russia it may be regarded as a mere "formality."

This means that a given document, though formally required, in effect signifies nothing.

An American professor received an invitation from one of the faculties of Moscow University to give a lecture there. He was awaited with eagerness. The details had been arranged and agreed at all levels of the organization.

The formal invitation necessary for him to be granted a visa was issued by a secretary and signed by one of the university bigwigs. Neither had heard of the professor, but all official documents had to be signed by a senior member of the board. As a result, a standard invitation was dispatched, containing quite different conditions from those agreed to. This upset the professor, who refused to come. The faculty staff sent him numerous faxes explaining that the invitation he had received was just a formal piece of paper necessary to obtain a visa, and that the conditions of his visit remained unchanged. In the end, the faculty staff also grew angry at the professor's lack of understanding.

There is a simple moral to this story: if something is out of order, clarify the issue first. It could simply be the carelessness of a secretary or minor bureaucrat, or the wrong document being sent to you. This can happen anywhere, but it is particularly likely to in Russia, where no one takes such documents seriously.

Often, not only are the instructions in it ignored, no one will even bother to read it.

Once your preparations have been completed, take a moment to reflect on the fact that the success of your undertaking depends largely on your readiness to understand the Russian point of view. Russian businessmen resent foreigners who come determined to play the game their own way, imposing their own rules of behavior when conducting negotiations. For example, American businessmen are sometimes considered to be too aggressive, overfamiliar, and lacking in delicacy.

WHEN TO GO

When planning a business trip to Russia you should take seasonal factors into account. Summer, which tends to be most popular with foreigners, is not the best time for business. It is the school and general holiday season, when all are intent on escaping from the stuffy cities into the countryside—whether at home or abroad. Even if your Russian partner agrees to meet you during summer, bear in mind that other staff members may well be on leave, and that your negotiations could be held up because the boss, without whose approval no final decision can be taken, has gone to Cyprus, or that the secretary, whose job it is to stamp the documents, is at her *dacha* planting potatoes.

It is not advisable to come to Russia a week before, during, or after a holiday. The busiest holiday period in Russia is the New Year. For two weeks before January 1 no one is in the mood for serious undertakings—there is too little time and therefore it is not worth starting anything. Office celebrations never coincide, and the whole period becomes one extended junket. People are preoccupied with buying presents, stocking up food, or solving domestic and family problems. On January 7 the Russians celebrate the Russian Orthodox Christmas, and on January 14, the so-called Old New Year. This is not an official holiday, yet many people observe it.

Family plays a major role in Russian life, and you should avoid the school holidays (November 1–10, December 30–January 11, and the last week in March). Many tough businessmen become meek as lambs when their offspring clamor to be taken to the sea or countryside.

The fall and, however paradoxical this may sound, the winter (with the exception of the New Year holiday period) are the best times for business trips to Russia. Only don't forget your fur hat and gloves!

BUSINESS MEETINGS AND NEGOTIATIONS

Negotiations in Russia are conducted in the office and only in the office. Inviting a colleague to a hotel suite for a formal business meeting is simply not done. This would cause confusion and be seen as lack of seriousness. Business lunches and even breakfasts are becoming more common, but only as a supplement to the main office-based meeting. However, Russians will actually talk about business everywhere—at a meal in a restaurant, at a private home where you are a guest, in the countryside over a barbecue, during an excursion to a museum, around the stove at a *dacha,* and so on. The end of the working day does not mean the end of work for a Russian, particularly if he is excited about a new project. Though your Russian colleague may be drunk, his discussion of your mutual cooperation will be lucid and to the point. Take note of what he says and ask questions. However, the next day clarify the points on which you have reached agreement once more. Many important issues in Russia are decided in an informal environment. Final agreement, though, may be reached only in the office.

TIMING AND PUNCTUALITY

In Russia, to be late for a meeting, even a business meeting, is not considered rude or a sign of disrespect. Certainly, the major Russian companies try to conduct negotiations within precise time limits, but in smaller firms you will, more likely than not, come up against disruptions to the timetable. The Russians have a different attitude to time, and a delay of ten to fifteen minutes is not regarded as being late at all.

Be Prepared to Wait

An American professor was invited to a meal in a Russian home and it was arranged that he meet his hostess at the Metro exit at 7:00 p.m. When she arrived at the appointed spot at twenty past seven, after work, having collected her child from the kindergarten and waited in line for a bus, the American was nowhere to be seen! With that, their acquaintance ended, for the professor considered that for his hostess to be late was unforgivable, while his hostess regarded his refusal to wait twenty minutes for her as bad manners.

So if you arrive at a meeting that is delayed because your Russian partners have not yet appeared, don't be upset. Incidentally, you, as a foreigner, will be expected to be punctual. The Russian attitude to time is reflected in the way they conduct negotiations, which can extend way beyond the time allotted to them. If your intentions are serious don't hurry, don't fuss, relax, and most important, don't schedule your appointments too closely together.

SENIORITY IN RUSSIAN BUSINESS

The beginning of a negotiation is very important. The Russian side will be introduced by the head of the organization or his deputy, in which case the deputy will always introduce his boss first. Introductions are often made in order of diminishing importance. Other variants, however, are possible, such as going around the table. In this case, the person making the introductions will almost certainly explain what he is doing, so that no one gets upset. Often women are introduced first, irrespective of rank. The same goes for elderly people, even if their presence at the negotiating table is purely formal, in order to emphasize their importance or so that they should not feel left out.

At the beginning of the twentieth century, Anton Chekhov described the "wedding generals," strangers who for a small sum were invited to a wedding, dressed up in uniform and medals, to impart an air of solemnity to the occasion. Today, too, people will often be invited to be present at negotiations who play no part in the making of

OBSERVING THE HIERARCHY

Failure to observe the pecking order on the
Russian side may cause seriously ruffled
feathers and be seen as a mark of disrespect
on your part. Here are some pointers to help
you avoid this.

• Meetings are usually held in the office of the
most senior-ranking member of those
present, though there is no guarantee that it
is he who will make the final decision.

• The boss usually sits at the head of the table,
and the rest often in order of diminishing
importance. The further away you are from
the boss, the less important your rank. The
secretary, as a rule, serves tea by seniority.

• If you understand Russian, listen to how
members of the Russian delegation address
each other. "*Vy*" (the formal "you") plus
Christian name-patronymic (as in "*Vy Victor
Vasilievich*") is a junior addressing a senior.
"*Ty*" (the informal "you") plus Christian
name (say, "*Ty Victor*") is used by a senior
addressing a junior.

- Even if you don't know the Russian language, observe how the Russians react to each other, who is asked the most questions, who is looked at most, and follow their intonation. Respect, as a rule, is detectable even without understanding the words.

- On the whole, it is better not to pay anyone, apart from the boss, too much attention. Even if you find what his deputy says to be more interesting, it is best to talk to him afterward, alone, outside his boss's office. Going out of your way to show consideration and respect for the leader of the Russian side is not just routine good manners. It is on his opinion that the success of the negotiations depends.

- For all that, attention to the middle and lower ranks of personnel can be very important. A lot depends on them—meetings, organization, and even the outcome of negotiations. A small souvenir and a bit of polite attention will, in the majority of cases, help your cause. Every Russian knows that often it is more important to please the secretary than her boss.

decisions but who, in the opinion of the Russian side, lend weight and a sense of respectability to the proceedings. Some of those present may not be introduced at all. This means they are either minor officials, or totally extraneous to the discussion. You should be prepared for the fact that a presence at the negotiating table does not necessarily imply interest in the talks.

As far as your delegation is concerned, the senior member of the party should speak first and do the introductions, presenting all the members of his team, describing their function and position, and indicating the degree of importance of each in the making of decisions. It is best immediately to inform your Russian counterparts about yourself, the aim of your visit, and about the nature of the documents you plan to sign.

For all the outward appearance of strict hierarchy in the Russian team, the internal relationships between its members are more fluid and democratic than you might think; relations between the boss and his subordinates will often be closer and less formal than is the case in the U.S.A. or the U.K. In Russia, the work collective used to be seen as a large family whose head, though possessing great power and authority, was still a member of the family. Although many companies emulate Western management practice, the old relationships still hold.

MEETING AND GREETING

In Russia, it is customary to start any meeting with an exchange of cards (the business card is regarded as an indicator of status, and position in society). An expensive, dark suit will make a positive impression on your Russian counterparts. On the other hand, there is a popular Russian saying that goes, "You are judged by your appearance first, but by your mind later on."

On meeting and parting in Russia it is customary to shake hands firmly with everyone around you, each time you meet, even if the negotiations continue for several days. Women are the exception here. Only shake hands when you meet them for the first time. Incidentally, in Russia it is considered gallant to kiss a woman's hand. Businesswomen should see this as a mark of respect, not as an indication of a cavalier attitude toward the "weaker" sex.

BUSINESS GIFTS

The Russians like receiving presents and, to some extent, expect them; they also love giving presents, so you may find yourself in an embarrassing position if you arrive empty-handed. Only ten years ago small souvenirs that symbolized the forbidden Western world were greatly appreciated. Today this type of present would be humiliating. Small gifts bearing the company logo should be given as a formality and not as anything special. The Russians are very sensitive about being treated with respect. It is better to give nothing—you'll simply be thought inconsiderate and it will be put down to cultural difference— than to give a worthless present that will earn you the reputation of stinginess and breed distrust.

It is a good idea to give one prestigious official present. This could be an item reflecting local characteristics or bearing the logo of your company. It should be big enough to be able to be displayed in the office. It is worth talking it up when presenting it. For instance, you might bring it into a speech about contacts between countries or cooperation between companies. As far as individual presents are concerned, men always appreciate alcoholic drinks (spirits are best, or drinks typical of your country), and women, chocolates, and everyone likes high-quality stationery items or accessories—fountain pens, leather folders, briefcases. The quality and cost of your presents should match the size of your company and the scale of the proposed project.

It is best to give your presents at the end or in the middle of negotiations, but not right away— first you need to get to know each other. Show gratitude for and make the right noises about the gift you have been given, even if they seem to you to be unnecessary, bulky, or cheap. It is quite possible that a lot of effort has gone into getting them. And yes, you can open them on receipt.

THE NEGOTIATION

Your Russian negotiating partners will be experienced in negotiation. They may also be specialized in the technical areas related to the discussion, but most important, they will be "chess players." In other words they plan several moves ahead. Your team should think of the consequences of each move before you make it.

Behind the Russian team is a hierarchy of decision makers that may include government or public departments. Many projects involving outside contractors have part government or mayoral shareholding. This constrains the negotiating freedom of the team, who may have to refer proposals back up the line for a decision. It also means that there may be reasons for doing things in a particular way that depend on undisclosed outside factors. The Russian team will speak with one voice and may experience confusion at the American and British tendency to express themselves as individuals, and even to allow internal disagreement to surface on tactical issues or matters of detail.

Being very hierarchical and status minded, they will expect you to be the same. The leveling jokes and familiarity of some American and British negotiators is totally out of place in Russia.

HOW MEETINGS PROCEED

The Russians normally expect you to speak first so that they can reflect on your position. It will be helpful if you have already prepared a document outlining your aims and how you hope to achieve them. They will present a draft outlining their starting position. Your draft should contain a number of throwaway points that can be conceded later without loss to your central argument. Your opening speech doesn't need to be specific. General statements of intent are appropriate. Part of Russian status consciousness is sensitivity to condescension. It is important that at no point should people feel talked down to.

Westerners generally prefer to proceed by agenda points. The Russian approach is less structured. They may not have an agenda at all, or if they do, they may not take the points in order.

They take a global rather than a step-by-step approach to the discussion, and the meeting may be quite informal by Western standards. This can lead to difficulties later in working out details and in the eventual implementation.

The Russian opening position may be expressed theatrically and vigorously and will clearly express their intent. They may talk at length. It's important not to show impatience. Use the opportunity instead to study your opposite numbers and work out the pecking order.

One issue for foreigners negotiating in Russia may be the use of "tough tactics." The Russians regard willingness to compromise as a sign of weakness. If there is a deadlock, the traditional Russian tactic is to show great patience and to "sit it out." One of the most famous exponents of the tactic, Stalin's foreign minister Molotov, was nicknamed "stonebottom" for this very quality. They will only abandon this tactic if you show considerable firmness, and concessions will only be made in return for concessions by the other side. This is why it is important to have some throwaway concessions in your original proposal. They may even make minor concessions and ask for major ones in return, and are suspicious of anything that is conceded easily.

The issue of firmness is an interesting one. Some Western negotiators prefer patience. Others prefer

THE IMPORTANCE OF PERSONAL RELATIONSHIPS

The Russians, above all, are people-oriented rather than deal-oriented. Their priorities are personal relationships, respect (form and status), and money. They are quite capable of walking away from a deal if the personal relationships feel wrong.

- Showing your human side is really important. At difficult moments personal relationships come into play and can help overcome deadlocks.
- As with Latin people, it is important to stress family closeness and show pictures of children. People will relate to your feelings, hopes, and aspirations more than to your commercial goals. In the meeting room the table may be laden with drink and food. This is an expression of hospitality. Eating and drinking with your negotiating partners is an important way of building up personal relationships.
- Be careful about complimenting individuals. If you single out an individual for special attention it can arouse envy and jealousy. If

you are going to pay attention to anybody, it has to be the boss. Try to find out who will sign the contract and make sure to establish personal contact with them.

- When showing firmness it is important to let a glimmer of kindness show through (in other words never forget your human side). You will find the Russians do the same, while being very direct. Remember that physical touching by Russians is a sign of confidence in you.

- The Russians are cautious and don't accept change easily. They are also suspicious of directives and regulations. If you can present necessary procedures as tried and tested personal recommendations, rather than official policy, they will be accepted more easily.

- There is a distrust of legal formulae and of officialdom. Right and wrong is decided by majority, not by law, and outcomes are achieved through personal relationships. They expect no help from the authorities.

- We have seen that the Russians are patriotic and like to hear praise of their national heroes and their technical and artistic achievements. They are very sensitive about war. For them wars are defensive, not aggressive. Keep your moral scruples to yourself.

to match toughness with toughness. There is some evidence to suggest that the Cuban missile crisis of 1961 was caused in part by President Kennedy's calmness in his meetings with Soviet Premier Khrushchev during earlier discussions. To put it crudely, Khrushchev decided the young Kennedy was a pushover. Only during the thirteen days of the crisis when Kennedy showed his steel was a compromise reached and the crisis solved.

A final point about agreements. The real agreement for a Russian is the verbal agreement based on mutual understanding between the partners. They do not appreciate armies of lawyers and ironclad contracts. Indeed, the Russians take the Oriental attitude to a contract. It is valid as long as it is beneficial to both parties. If circumstances change, then they are within their rights to ask for it to be amended.

MANAGING DISAGREEMENT

Dealing with disagreement should be done, as far as possible, in personal rather than official terms. While it is important to understand where authority lies and to work within that structure, do not take a legalistic approach. Disagreement will usually be obvious, but may be expressed obliquely, as in "We'll have to see what we can do."

Avoid hurting people's pride and don't throw

the book at them. Always take personal feelings into account and deal with disagreement openly and verbally rather than in writing. This may best be done outside office hours.

It is also important if you are in a position of authority to show firmness and leadership. Remember that early compromise may be seen as a sign of weakness. It is helpful to monitor people and not to disappoint them once they have put their trust in you. The Russians respect authority, and once trust is given it is vital to honor it.

Remember, too, that perceptions and feelings are more important than facts, and that what people are seeking is not necessarily an edge over you but an acceptable way of working through difficult circumstances. Historically, Russia's best means of defense has been attack. Remember this in a standoff. Show that you understand their difficulties, do not hide your own difficulties, and generally be direct and straightforward.

INTERPRETING

A word about interpreters is useful. Regardless of the ability of the participants to speak English, large official meetings will be held in both Russian and English. The Russians consider their language to be on a par with English, and in set-piece deliberations will expect to use it.

It is important to take shorthand notes of the proceedings as a record of what has occurred and as a way of checking that all relevant points have been agreed upon. The note-taker should understand Russian well as Russian nuances may be lost in translation.

When speaking through an interpreter make sure to use short sentences. Use the active voice and simple words and idioms as far as possible. Pause frequently and tell the interpreter when to proceed. Remember that to translate an average English sentence into Russian needs roughly 10 percent more words and time.

In speaking and listening through an interpreter it is important to focus on the Russian speaker, not the interpreter. Remember that the Russian is looking at your body language to assess your reaction. You should do the same.

CONTRACT FINALIZATION

The Russians like to put in writing any agreement that has been reached and how it will be implemented. This document is called a *protocol,* or memorandum of understanding. It serves the same function as a letter of intent; it has no legal force but is a statement of what has been agreed to. When the final contract is drawn up in English and in Russian, each draft will be compared and where there is no disagreement in wording the drafts will be underlined. Where there is disagreement the offending lines will be bracketed and will be returned for further discussion.

CONCLUSION

The Russians are both relationship-minded and sharp business negotiators, and don't see a conflict between the two. They will use both their personal charm and their hard-nosed commercial experience on you. You should be able to do the same. Above all, remember that respect for seniority and leadership is important in Russian society. It is important to avoid giving offense by not showing the right degree of respect. It is also important not to forego the respect that is due to you. Not always an easy balancing act, but as they say in Russia, "You should always be thinking."

chapter nine

COMMUNICATING

Communications in Russia leave much to be desired. Certainly the postal system is erratic and should not be used for important documents.

MAIL

Letters can be sent from any post office or from the blue mail boxes in the street. If you are mailing a letter overseas, ask for a *mezhdunarodny* (international) envelope. If it isn't printed with the sign AVIA (Airmail) you should also get an airmail sticker. For anything important use courier services. Fedex, TNT, and DHL all have offices in many Russian cities.

If you are sending correspondence to or within Russia remember to write the address in Russian. Letters addressed in English are, for obvious reasons, harder to deliver than those in Cyrillic script. The postal service is one of those areas of Russian life badly in need of reform.

When addressing letters titles are normally avoided. A letter addressed to, say, the Foreign

Trade Academy in Moscow, might read like this:

Name	Marina Balashova
Organization	Foreign Trade Academy
Postcode and city	119285 Moscow
Street	Pudovkin Str., 4A
Country	Russia

The telephone number would be written like this:
Tel. (095) 148-44-99

Private addresses may have two numbers. These may refer to a building on the corner of two streets. Thus 4/3 would mean that 4 is on the main street and 3 on the cross-street. Groups of buildings may be numbered 4, 4a, 4b, etc. This happens when they are situated close to each other but do not front on to the main street (for example, when they are built inside the block). The block may also have a name and an entrance number, for example Korpus 2, and the apartment (*kvartira*) number will be shown as Kv. 10. Private addresses may not contain a postcode.

TELEPHONE
As in many other countries the problems, expense, and delays of getting a landline means that the Russians have jumped a generation and gone

straight to cell phones. Cell phones in Russia work on the European principle, and you will need a tri-band or European cell phone to make calls. As far as landlines are concerned, numbers are presented like this.

Country	Area code	Number
07	095 (Moscow)	138 34 45
07	812 (St. Petersburg)	138 34 45

To phone from Russia, dial the exit code for your hotel or company, then 8, then 10, followed by the country code. Thus a call to Manhattan might be:

Outside city	8
Outside Russia	10
US country code	1
Area code	212 (New York)
Number	234 678

(You would dial 00 for abroad only on special digital lines, in Western-style offices for example.)

In many areas of Russian life the legacy of the Soviet Union dies hard. An example of this is the reluctance of people to take responsibility for answering telephones, taking messages, and responding to messages left on answering machines. This means that, unless you can get straight through to your contact, you may run into difficulties if you leave messages and wait for a response. The best strategy is to keep calling.

The Russian telephone system itself is not helpful to communication. Even if the end you're calling from is high-tech, the receiving end may not be. Therefore missed calls, being cut off in mid call, or wrong numbers, may be a daily if not hourly occurrence. Faxes can be equally frustrating. The city of St. Petersburg solved the problem by forming an early alliance with a Western supplier, and has a reasonably modern system that works. Do not expect the same in Moscow or elsewhere.

THE INTERNET

The Internet is therefore a very important means of communication. A five-pronged telephone plug is used, and you will need to get a tele-adaptor set before you leave home. Although gateways can be a problem—because of credit-card fraud some Internet Service Providers have closed down in Russia—there are very many Internet cafés in the big cities, and in the regions, offering easy access to Yahoo, Hotmail, and the like. Note that if you are looking for Web sites in Russia the code is "ru."

The Net is growing in importance in Russia. President Putin himself conducted an interactive Internet broadcast with the aim of encouraging

Russians to make more use of the medium. Despite its considerable achievements in science and the high level of literacy, only a fraction of Russia's population currently uses the Internet.

Interestingly, on the webcam Putin himself appeared unflatteringly short and had a modest manner. He didn't surround himself with the props of power and he didn't try to appear tough. The tough Putin is reserved for his policies. He claimed he didn't push for the Presidency, and maintained that his wife wore the trousers at home and controlled their daughters when they spent too much time on the Net. A very different image from that projected by his predecessors.

FINDING OUT WHAT IS GOING ON

The best source of local news and information in English is the English-language newspapers such as the *Moscow Times* or the *St. Petersburg Times*. These can be accessed on www.themoscowtimes.ru, or www.thepetersburgtimes.ru.

To find out what the Russians are talking about you can always look at the pictures of the main Russian newspapers. The press in Russia has been in constant flux since 1991, due partly to frequent changes of ownership and partly to a degree of suppression by the government (couched as anti-corruption rather than political repression).

Television

In the bad old days Russian TV had four channels, all state run. If you channel-hopped, a popular Russian joke went, you would see the same thing on all three channels, and if you surfed to the fourth, a KGB colonel appeared on the screen to say, "Stop channel surfing, or else . . . !"

Nowadays the state once again controls the four TV channels. ORT is the name of Russian public television. The last independent national channel, TVC, was liquidated by the Supreme Arbitration Court. The four state channels are thus the main source of information for the country, since only 6 percent of the population uses the Internet and the print media are too expensive for most Russians.

Foreign Media

The Russians still don't trust their own media. A typical Russian joke goes, "Will swap two TV sets for one radio that receives foreign stations." Many hotels subscribe to international satellite services and foreign visitors have access to CNN and Eurosport, and in some hotels to BBC World and NBC. The best source of outside radio news is still the BBC World Service, transmitting on short wave or on 648m medium wave. You can find out details by accessing www.bbc.co.uk.

The Press

Even if you can't understand them yourself, it is helpful to be familiar with the main Russian newspapers so that when colleagues and friends mention them, you know what they are referring to. These are *Rossiiskaya Gazeta* (government sponsored), *Pravda, Izvestia,* and *Kommercant* (business). The Russian News Agency is called TASS.

GREETINGS

For anyone apprehensive about the traditional Russian bearhug and kisses on both cheeks, fear not. The traditional Russian greeting is shaking hands, and bearhugs are reserved for close friends and relatives. The Russians are not afraid of showing emotions. If a meeting goes well you can expect strong handshakes, and back slapping, including bearhugs, may be an indication of a very successful outcome. Lack of warm contact can be a sign of something wrong.

BODY LANGUAGE

The Russians will often use body language rather than verbal expression to show their feelings.

People may wink or nod to show a positive attitude. Remember, too, that smiling is not an automatic social response, as it is among the

Americans and British, but is a clear indication of approval. Laughing is different. A Russian sales executive watching an amusing sales presentation felt it was important to say, "Just because we are laughing does not mean that we approve of it!"

Strong eye contact in Russia is an indication of sincerity. Looking away or failing to meet the eye is considered a sign of deviousness.

Like the Germans and the French, the Russians expect to shake hands at the beginning and end of meetings. Unlike the Germans and the French, they often don't offer to do so with women. If a women offers her hand, however, the Russians will respond.

Hand gestures are common, but the Russians don't point or wag fingers across a table. And don't raise two fingers in the V-sign. In Russia it may be mistaken for "Up yours!"

Personal Space

The Russians have less need for personal space than the Americans or British, and listening to, or even joining in, other people's conversations is not unusual. Russian has no word for privacy. This is reflected in the way people barge through crowds in subways or board buses and trains. Don't get upset. It is not intentionally rude.

STYLES OF COMMUNICATION

On the whole American and British people are concise in their style of expression. They say what they have to say, and are careful not to go on too long. The Russians, by contrast, may come across as long-winded. Explaining things in detail is an aspect of Russian thoroughness, and if uninterrupted can take a long time. However, if they can have their say uninterrupted, they will be much more disposed to listen to you.

NORMALNO!

Is it natural Russian pessimism that prevents them from getting too upset in a crisis? What foreigners describe as Russian stoicism, the Russians describe as *normalno* (normal), suggesting that for them crisis management, or at least riding out crises, is a fact of life.

Business As Usual

After the Russian banking crash in the 1990s, Prime Minister Viktor Chernomyrdin is reported to have said, "We thought things would be all right but as usual they turned out as normal."

PRIDE

The Russians are proud. This means that you don't tell jokes against Russia. They can, but you shouldn't. Pride extends to not embarrassing people in public. Don't say, "You've got to be joking," or "You're wrong!" It is important to find a face-saving way for them to back down in a disagreement or crisis. Finally, do not broach subjects they think best buried, including much of recent history. If the occasion is right and you are interested, they will raise them themselves.

SWEARING

You might expect that an exuberant, emotional, hard-drinking people would not have problems with swearwords. On the contrary, the Russians can be unexpectedly restrained in this respect, especially in front of women. Swearing is associated with hooliganism. Avoid it.

OPENING UP

We've seen that attitudes toward foreigners are complicated. Some Russians believe that all foreigners, and Americans in particular, live the enviable lives of characters in a soap opera. Others regard them with contempt, seeing them as mercenary, unprincipled, uneducated, and dull. However, having been deprived of contact with the outside world for so long, Russians are now seizing the opportunity to learn about it and to study foreign languages. A person who knows a foreign language is highly respected and is likely to get a better job.

English is the most popular foreign language in Russia. It is on the curriculum of most secondary schools and universities, and you are certain to hear a few simple English words or phrases from strangers in the street. German is the second-most popular language, followed by French.

However, the essential warmth of Russia goes beyond language. Mark Twain wrote that the world can be felt and understood without a language: "I talked to the Russians a good deal, just to be friendly, and they talked to me from the same motive; I am sure that both enjoyed the conversation, but never a word of it either of us understood."

CONCLUSION

Russia has gone through a difficult period since the fall of Communism. The great achievement has been personal freedom, but the great disappointments have been the failure to improve living standards and the slowness of reform. The Russians themselves are frustrated by the difficulties they have encountered when unleashing their natural enthusiasm and enterprise to rebuild their country. They need respect and empathy, and they see it in foreigners who are prepared to be complimentary about Russia, who are open and trustworthy, who will listen, and who are good company. With those qualities, you can succeed in the new Russia.

Appendix: The Cyrillic Alphabet

Street and Metro signs in Russia are in Cyrillic, so familiarity with the Russian alphabet is advisable. The following table gives the alphabet, in upper and lower case, with the standard forms of transliteration used in the United States and Britain.

А	а	a			
Б	б	b			
В	в	v			
Г	г	g			
Д	д	d			
Е	е	e	ye	je	ie
Ж	ж	zh	ž		
З	з	z			
И	и	i			
Й	й	ĭ			
	ий	y			
К	к	k			
Л	л	l			
М	м	m			
Н	н	n			
О	о	o			
П	п	p			
Р	р	r			
С	с	s			
Т	т	t			
У	у	u			
Ф	ф	f			
Х	х	kh	h		
Ц	ц	ts	c		
Ч	ч	ch	č		
Ш	ш	sh	š		
Щ	щ	shch	šč		
—	ъ	"			
—	ы	ȳ	y	ui	yi
	ый	uy			
	ь	'			
Э	э	é	è		
Ю	ю	yu	ju	iu	
Я	я	ya	ja	ia	

Further Reading

Figes, Orlando. *Natasha's Dance. A Cultural History of Russia.*
London: Penguin Books, 2002.

Freeland, Chrysia. *Sale of the Century.* London: Little Brown, 2000.

Gerem, Yves. *Moscow Guide.* New York: Open Road Publishing, 2000.

Hobson, Charlotte. *Black Earth City: A Year in the Heart of Russia.* London:
Granta Publications, 2001.

Holdsworth, Nick. *Moscow the Beautiful and the Damned.* London:
Andre Deutsch, 2000.

Hosking, Geoffrey. *Russia and the Russians.* London: Penguin Books, 2001.

Kapuscinski, Ryszard. *Imperium.* New York: Alfred A Knopf, 1993.

Klein, Lawrence R. *The New Russia.* Stanford: Stanford University Press, 2001.

Korotich, Vitaly. *The Best of Ogonyok.* London: Heinemann, 1990.

Kotkin, Stephen. *Armageddon Averted, The Soviet Collapse 1970-2000.*
Oxford: OUP, 2001.

Linehan, Paddy. *Trans-Siberia: Inside the Grey Area.* Chichester:
Summersdale Press, 2000.

McCauley, Martin. *Bandits, Gangsters and the Mafia.* London:
Longman, 2001.

Mitchell, Charles. *Passport Russia.* New York: World Trade Press, 1953.

Moynahan, Brian. *The Russian Century.* New York: Random House, 1994.

Reid, Anna. *The Shaman's Coat. A Native History of Siberia.*
London: Weidenfeld & Nicolson, 2002.

Richmond, Yale. *From Nyet to Da.* Yarmouth, Maine: Intercultural Press, 2003.

Ter-Minasova, Svetlana. *Language, Culture and Communication.*
Moscow: Moscow State University, 1995.

Ter-Minasova, Svetlana. *Language, Linguistics and Life.* Moscow:
Moscow State University, 1996.

Thomas, Bryn. *Trans-Siberian Handbook.* Hindhead: Trailblazer
Publications, 2001.

Time Out. *Time Out Moscow and St. Petersburg.* London:
Penguin Books, 1999.

White, Stephen. *Developments in Russian Politics 5.* Basingstoke:
Palgrave, 2001.

Russian. A Complete Course. New York: Living Language, 2005.

In-Flight Russian. New York: Living Language, 2001.

Index

alcohol 73-5, 92
Alexander II, Tsar 26
Alexander III, Tsar 26
Alexander Nevsky, Prince of
    Novgorod 20
apartments 113, 120
area 10
Armenia 15, 34
art 18, 24, 25, 48, 94-5
Astrakhan 22
Azerbaijan 9, 15

Baku, Azerbaijan 9
ballet 18, 95, 99, 102
Baltic states 8, 15, 33
banking 88-9, 125, 161
banya (bathhouse) 93-4
Basil III, Grand Duke of Moscow
    21
Batu Khan 20
Belarus (Belorussia) 8, 15, 18, 25,
    33
body language 158-9
Bolsheviks 29, 30
boyars (ancient princely families)
    21, 22
bribery 48
buses 117
Bush, George 33
business card 141
business culture 126-30
Byzantium 19, 23, 63

capitalism 35, 54
cars 84, 114-16
Catherine the Great 24-5
Chechnya 36
CheKa 29
children, attitudes to 90
Church and state 64-5
Churchill, Winston 12, 32
cinema 95-6
cities 10
climate 10, 13, 14, 40
Cold War 31-2, 33
collective farms (*kolkhoz*) 30, 42
collectivism 42, 44
Commonwealth of Independent
    States (CIS) 9, 15, 35
communal spirit 42-4
communication, styles of 160
Communism 37, 42, 54, 163
Communist Party 29, 30, 32, 37,
    38-9, 42, 99

concerts 95, 99
constitution (1993) 35-9
contract finalization 150-51
conversation 68-9, 75-6, 80
correspondence 46
Cossacks 21-2, 23, 25, 27
countryside 101
coup attempt (1991) 34, 35
credit cards 88
Crimea 25
cultural programs 102
currency 10, 16, 35, 36, 88-9, 92
Cyrillic alphabet 19, 23, 115,
    116, 164

dachas 83-4, 87, 93, 134, 135
Dagestan 36
Decembrists 26
democracy 37, 39, 54
Dimitry Donskoy, Prince of
    Muscovy 20
disagreement, managing 148-9
Dnieper River 19, 21
Dolgoruki, Grand Prince Yuri 98-9
Don River 20, 21
dress 79, 121
drinks 71-5, 79, 86
dual price system 55
Duma (elected parliament) 28, 34,
    35-6, 38, 39
dusha (soul) 56-7

Eastern (Asiatic or Pacific) Russia
    14, 15-16
economy 15, 16-17, 35, 36, 86-9,
    124-6
education 89-91
Eisenstein, Sergei 20, 22, 27
electricity 11
Estonia 8, 15, 33, 34, 35
ethnic makeup 11, 14
etiquette, business 130-31

family 50-52, 82
Far East, Russian 16, 27, 37, 124,
    125
Federal Council (*Soviet Federatsii*)
    38
finding your way 120-21
First World War 28
Five Year Plans 30
food 70-73, 80, 87, 92
foreigners, attitudes to 54-6,
    162

Genghis Khan 20
geography 13-14
Georgia 15, 34, 35
gift giving 49-50, 77-8, 79, 141-3
glasnost (openness) 32, 33
Golden Horde 20
Gorbachev, Mikhail 32-3, 34, 35
government 11, 37-9, 125
Grachev, General 34
greetings 158
gulags 31

health 121-2
hierarchy 49, 138-9
Hitler, Adolf 31
holidays 58-61, 134
hospitality and entertaining 69-73,
    79
    reciprocation 80-81
hotels 108-13

inflation 16, 35, 86, 125, 126
Internet 155-6
interpreting 149-50
invitations home 78-80
Irkutsk 14
Iron Curtain 32
Ivan the Fool 40-41
Ivan III (Ivan the Great) 21
Ivan IV (Ivan the Terrible) 22, 99

Kazakhstan 15, 21, 33, 35
Kazan 22
Kerensky, Alexander 29
KGB 29, 34
Khans 20
Khrushchev, Nikita 32, 41, 148
Kiev 19
Kievan Rus 8, 19
Kremlin, Moscow 98-9
Kulaks (peasant farmers) 28
Kuril Islands 16
Kyrgyzstan 15

Lake Baikal 14, 20
language 11, 12, 17, 162
Latvia 8, 15, 33, 34, 35
Lenin, Vladimir Ilyich 29, 30
Lenin Mausoleum, Moscow 100
literature 18, 68-9
Lithuania 8, 15, 25, 33, 34, 35
Livonian Knights 20

mail 152-3

Manchuria 14
markets 85, 96
media 11, 156, 157-8
meetings
    business 135
    how meetings proceed 144-5,
    148
    informal 81
military service 91
Moldova 8, 15, 34, 35
Mongols 20
Moscow 16, 17, 25, 27-8, 89, 95,
    98-100, 102
    capital moved to 29
    free time in 92
    Metro 101, 116-17
    museums 94-5
    rise of 20-21
    Russia's heart 23, 24, 98
museums 94-5
music 18

Napoleon Bonaparte 25-6
negotiations 135, 143-4
Neva River 20, 24
"New Russians" 17, 48, 51, 87,
    126-7
Nicholas I, Tsar 26
Nicholas II, Tsar 27, 28, 30
NKVD 29, 31
normalno (normal) 160-61
Novgorod 19, 21
nuclear weapons 33

Oligarchs 17
openness 32, 45-6, 47, 163
opera 95

parks 100
passport 107, 108
patriotism (*rodina*) 44, 69
perestroika (restructuring) 32
personal space 160
Peter I, Tsar (Peter the Great) 24
Peter III, Tsar 24
Petrograd *see* St. Petersburg
police 106, 115-16
population 11, 12, 16
Potemkin, Count Grigori 25
preparing for a visit 131-3
    when to go 133-4
prices 89
pride 161
protocols 108

Putin, Vladimir 37, 39, 65

Red Army 29-30, 31
Red Square, Moscow 99-100
Reds 29
regional politics 39
relationships 49-50, 146-7
religion 19, 23, 62-7
residence permit (*propiska*) 82-3
restaurants 81, 104-5
Romanov, Mikhail, Tsar 22-3
rules and regulations, attitude to 45
Rurik of Jutland 19
Rus clan 19
Russian civil war 30
Russian Federation 8, 15-17, 33, 39, 90
Russian Orthodox Church 19, 21, 62-5, 99
Russian Revolution (1905) 27-8
Russian Revolution (1917) 8, 15, 16, 23, 28-30, 50, 64
Russo-Japanese war 27

St. Basil's Cathedral, Moscow 99
St. Petersburg 16, 24, 25, 27-8, 29, 95, 100
    "White Nights" 14, 102
Sakhalin Island 16
Samara 37
Saratov 37
Second World War 22, 31
security 122-3
seniority 137, 140
serfdom 23, 25, 26-7
shaking hands 141, 158
shopping 84-5, 97-8
Siberia 14, 15, 16, 22, 65, 66, 124, 125
Slavs 18
smiling 53
Smolensk 19
Soviets 28
space travel 18
sport 103
Stalin, Joseph 30-31, 32
Stalingrad 31
steppes 14
Stolypin, Pyotr 28
subways 116-17
superstitions 63, 78
suspicion and secrecy 47
swearing 161

Tajikistan 15, 33
Tatars 20, 21, 22, 23
taxis 113-14
telephone 11, 153-5
television 11, 157
theater 95, 102
thinking big 56
time zones 10
timing and punctuality 135-7
toasts 74-5, 79-80
toilets 92
trains 118-19
Transcaucasia 33
Trotsky, Leon 29
Tsars 22-4, 26-8, 30, 37, 99
tundra 13, 14

Ukraine 8, 15, 18, 19, 25, 27, 35
Union of Soviet Socialist Republics (Soviet Union) 8, 15, 30-35
Ural Mountains 13, 14, 15
Uzbekistan 15, 33

vaccinations 122
vegetarians 73
video/TV 11
Vikings 19
visas 106-8
Vladivostok 14, 16, 27, 37, 125
Volga River 19, 31
Voltaire 25
Voronezh 14, 37

wages 55, 86, 87
walking 119-20
Warsaw Pact 32
wealth and money 47-8
weddings 59
Western (European) Russia 14, 15
White House, Moscow 34
Whites 29, 30
women, attitudes to 50-53

Yaroslav, Grand Prince 19
Yekaterinburg 14
Yeltsin, Boris 31, 33-7, 41, 65

Zemsky Zobor (Assembly of the Land) 22